Step·by·Step

Architectural Marker Techniques

Minoru Azuchi + AIR STUDIO

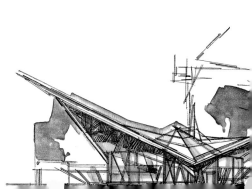

感性のダイレクト表現
三澤千代治

「ミサワプロジェクト」企画&デザイン：ミサワホーム株式会社 三澤千代治
Planning and design of "Misawa Project"： Misawa Homes Co., Ltd., Chiyoji Misawa

建造物の外観やインナー・スペース全体のプランニングも，設計図やスケッチ表現共にコンピュータ化しつつあるというコンピュータ全盛の現状の中で，これからのパースの方向性の質と内容が問われることは確実である。

これからのスペースプロジェクトのイメージ・プレゼンテーションが，より人間環境の感性にマッチさせる表現が必要とされ，そのプランニングの段階での表現方法として，人間の生の手による，より高い感性での表現を探るべきであるということである。

人間の感性による，より感覚的に訴えるプランニングとモノ作りこそが，人間環境を中心に置いた空間として求められる姿である。今後のスペース・レンダリングの向かうべき方向は，まさにその意味を包括した作品でなければならないということである。

ここに掲載したプロジェクト『ミサワプロジェクト』もこのような感性の表現をモットーとして，イメージし表現した作品のひとつである。このイメージ・レンダリングの中には，コンピュータではまだまだ描くことのできない，かなり人間臭い感覚的な表現によるイメージが描かれている。直感的に描いていく一本一本のライン，そしてひとつひとつの違ったタッチの表現の集積により，感性豊かな作品に仕上げていくわけである。植物をはじめとする，水のせせらぎ，乱舞する鳥やチョウなどの自然の精と，その中で楽しく会話を楽しむ人々のざわめきと流れる音楽が，美しいハーモニーをかもしだす。このような表現方法によって，この空間にはファッション性とアート感覚が生まれ，従来のパースではなかなか表現しきれなかったあたらしい作品が誕生する。

この描法をさらに容易にさせる方法は，描き手の感性の豊かさもさるこ

とながら，思いついた感性をよりダイレクトに，そして新鮮に表現できるマーカーの存在が大きいといえる。

「夢のあるプロジェクト」は，それがスケールが大きくなればなるほど，人間社会の感性に与える直接的な影響は大きく，ある意味では，社会の中で大変重要な役割を担っているともいえる。

スペース・プランニングの中で，単にコンピュータやデータによるプロジェクトが創造されようとしている現代では，あまりにも造形デザインのみにこだわってみたり，奇をてらってみたりした，人間不在のデザインが多すぎるきらいがあるように思われる。

つまり，人間がこれから創造するものの中で，最も大切なことは，ここ数十年の間に起きた表面的な情報ではなく，過去何百，何千年もの歴史の中で培って来た，音楽家や画家などによる感覚の世界の中にこそ重要な無限のファクターが現存し，表現されているといっても過言ではない。さらに，バッハやモーツアルトの音楽，レオナルド・ダ・ビンチや北斎，マチスなどの絵画の中には，どんなスーパー・コンピュータでもかなわない無限の人間による，人間の感性に訴えかける，感覚的情報が表現されているということである。

このように，アートや音楽にも通じる豊かな感性こそが，これからの未来の空間デザインの創造に，より直接的につながっていかなければならない。その意味で，人間性あふれた表現により近いイメージのプレゼンテーションが，今後更に重要になっていくと思う。

Direct Expressions Of One's Sense

Chiyoji Misawa

We are now in the midst of the computer age where planning of external appearences and the entire inner space of buildings, as well as creating blueprints and rough sketches are all computerized. Consequently, there is no doubt that architectural rendering in future will depict the better quality and substance.

This means that the image presentation of space projects will require an expression that will match to one's sense for living enviroments.It is essential for renderers to understand that the environment presented through the architectural rendering is entirely for one's pleasant life. The work of future space rendering should, therefore, naturally include this concept. The "Misawa Project", covered in this chapter is one of the projects of which the expression was based on such understanding. The images rendered here contain such sensible expressions which computers are notyet employed. Every line drawn by instinct, every different touch of expressions is carefully selected to complete these illustrations as rich and sensible works.

Murmuring of water, exhilarating birds and butterflies, voices of people enjoying their conversation, and flowing music is harmonized together and one can feel a pleasant atmosphere through the illustrations. Such methods can achieve a fashionable and artistic sense of space which is unattainable in the rendering methods in the past. This

brings forth a new type of art with each work.

This method of drawing becomes easier if the artist has a right understanding and rich sensibility, but it can also play a large role for those who use marker as this media can express their plans directly and vividly.

Unfortunately there are too many designs that stick to formative methods, and some people try to show off small oddities or omit human items in the space planning of the modern age when the creation of the project is to be input as data into a computer (commonsense data is the past).

In fact, the thing we need to value from now on as we attend to the creative work is not the superficial data of the past few decades, but the unlimited amount of data and factors which have been highly valued by musicians and painters for hundreds and thousands of years. This means that the unlimited and sensible information created by people and appealing to the sense of human beings is expressed in the music of Bach and Mozart and in the artwork of Leonardo Da Vinci, Hokusai and Matisse, and these could not have been produced by computers. It is these rich sensations which are understood in the fields of art and music which have to have a direct linkage to the creation of future space design. In this sense, the image presentation which is akin to the expression filled with humane nature will become a more important element in the future.

目 次
Contents

感性のダイレクト表現
Direct Expressions Of One's Sense

0 0 2

第 一 章
色彩と雰囲気を中心にしたイメージ・コンセプトスケッチ
Chapter 1
Color Application and Expression of the Atmosphere of Subjects.

0 1 5

第 二 章
空間と形態を中心にしたイメージ・コンセプトスケッチ
Chapter 2
The Expression of Space, Perspective, and Form.

0 4 5

第 三 章
現代的なリアル・イメージスケッチ
Chapter 3
How to Employ A Realistic Touch to Subjects.

0 8 5

第 四 章
コピーフリーの点景ファイル集
Chapter 4
Copyright-free Spot Images.

1 3 7

あとがき
Afterword

1 5 0

プロセスの前に，マーカーの特性と使い方について

まず，マーカーの一番の特性は，表現がダイレクトであること。
ダイレクト性，これである。
描けるスピードも速いし，乾かす必要もない。どんどん描ける。
水彩やエアブラシ，不透明水彩などの何倍もの速さで描ける。
そして最近はかなりの色の数と種類が発売されているので，
速いうえに，かなりの描き込みが可能になった。
私が考えるには，ある意味ではコンピューターグラフィックの表現と
双璧の可能性を秘めている現代の表現だと思われる。
半世紀前にはなかった表現である。
他の画材に比べて，発色が非常にいい。
軽快感が現代の表現に合っている。
しかし，トーンの重ねぐあいによって，
それなりの重さ，深さも表現できるようになった。
他の画材（水彩，鉛筆）などと組み合わせて描くと，
また違った表現ができる。
この画材をうまく使いこなす一番のこつは，色を選ぶとき，
1色1色をじっくり考えて選ぶこと。
なぜならば，他の画材と違って，修正が非常に難しいからだ。
まず，1枚のパースを描く前に全体の色を決め，

どのマーカーで描くかが，パースのプロセスのスピードを速める。
色が決まり，マーカーで画面を描くときは，いっきに，
そしてスピーディに途中でまようことなく，
1本のタッチで描くことが必要だ。そしてこのタッチを描くリズム，
これこそがマーカーパースを描くテクニックで一番重要なことなのだ。
このリズムが，マーカーのタッチのリズムになり画面に精気をあたえ，
新鮮さと軽快感をあたえる。
こまかなテクニックより一番重要なことが，ここにある。
もたもたしていたり，まよったりしていると，
せっかくのマーカーの特色が，まるで生かされなくなるであろう。
あまり，こまかな失敗は気にせず，
しかし繊細にスピーディーに描けるようになれば，
マーカーのよりいい表現が，できると思われる。
ある意味では，非常に簡単で，誰にでもできる表現であるが，
一方では非常に味わいが深く，
テクニックがどんどん無限に見えてくる画材でもある。
いずれにしても，まずは，自分で楽しく描くことが重要である。
良き音楽でも聞きながら…。

The specialties and methods of marker work prior to process.

The first thing that one must remember about the special characteristics of markers is that it is possible to express oneself directly. This is a real advantage as it enables one to draw swiftly and negates the necessity of waiting for the paint to dry. They are also extremely easy to use. The speed of the work is increased several times over more conventional materials such as water colors, air-brushes and opaque paint, and with the recent burdgeoning of the available colors it is more and more possible to draw in great detail. It is my view that markers add a kind of modern expression that is only equalled by computer graphics, both of which will stand out like twin stars.
Such expression was attainable half a century ago, and the colors came out well in comparison to other painting materials. The light touch of the marker suits the modern expression, and it has now become possible to further express the heaviness and depth of a picture in its own way by adjusting the arrangement of the tones.
Additionally, one can produce different styles of work by combining the marker with other painting materials such as water colors and pencils.
The secret of mastering this tool is hidden in the time spent selecting the colors before use as alterations are very difficult to make in comparison with other painting materials. Initially a rough idea of the overall color scheme should be decided and then the colors themselves should be placed in order of use before commencing a perspective work. This will quicken the process of the work.
Marker paintings should be approached with single decisive strokes that move swiftly without hesitation. It is the rhythm of these strokes that is considered the most important technique in the production of perspectives by markers. This rhythm will add an impression of spirit and swing to the picture. It is thought that this is more important than any other technique.
The special charactistics of markers will be lost if one is a slow or hesitant worker. The creation of better marker works will be attained if one manages to overcome worrying about small mistakes and concentrates on a confident and speedy style of detail drawing. On one hand the marker can be a very simple and easy tool to work with, but, on the other hand, it can be complicated and difficult as there is an endless array of techniques available.
Anyway, the most important thing is to enjoy drawing. Why not try it with a piece of good music playing in the background？

	テーマ Theme	ポイント Points
Project 1	全体の雰囲気，空気感の表現。 The entire atmosphere, The expression of the air.	グレー系，モノトーンは不使用。 パステルトーン中心の自由なマーカーの表現。 Shades of grey. Monotones are not used. Free marker expression with pastel tones.
Project 2	空間や形を色のグラデーション，バリエーションによって表現。 The space and shapes are expressed by the use of color graduation and variation.	マーカーの色の塗り重ねにより，画面の中で， 色のバリエーションを表現。 The color variation within the picture is expressed by an over-coat of markers.
Project 3	モノトーンによる質感，空間の表現。 The quality of the materials and space is expressed by the use of monotones.	描く質感によって，マーカーやその他の画材の 使用テクニックの違い。 The usage and techniques of markers and other painting materials vary in accordance to the quality of the drawing.
Project 4	ガラス，ステンレスなどのハイテックで硬質な素材の表現。 The expression of hard materials with a degree of high technology such as glass and stainless steel.	直線的タッチとブルー系，寒色系を中心とした表現。 A lineal touch and cool colors are used to express the hard materials.
Project 5	Project 4のバリエーションで，色を鮮やかで派手にした表現。 This is a variation of Project 4 with brighter colors.	画面上での色彩バランスのとり方。 The color balance within the picture.
Project 6 **Project 7** **Project 8** **Project 9**	おのおののコーナーの空間のテーマの違いを，同じ質感で描き分ける。 質感は木調，石，布，コンクリート打ちっぱなし， ミラーなど内装パースの一般的テクニックで表現。 The different themes of the space in each corner should be drawn differently from an image of the same quality. The quality materials such as wood, stone, cloth, concrete and hammered mirrors should be expressed by using the general techniques of interior perspective drawing.	構図の違いによる各コーナーの描き方の違い。 木調，布などのやわらかい素材の描き方のポイント。 コンクリート打ちっぱなし，石などの表現。 The various drawing methods of each corner using different painting compositions. The drawing points of soft materials such as wood and cloth. The expressions of reinforced concrete and stone.
Project 10 **Project 11** **Project 12** **Project 13**	一つの作品で，内装と外装を描き分ける。 Draw the interior and exterior decorations.	

パースの様式，方向性について
With regards to the style and directionalism of perspective drawings.

近未来風な表現。
The immediate future expression.

●ハイテックな表現。（金属，ガラス他）
— High technological expression.

●リアルな表現。（ネオクラシズム）
● Realistic expression (neo-classisism).

色彩について
With regard to coloring.

色彩の色味による
ダイレクトな表現。
Direct expression
through color tastes.

●モノトーン，
茶系が入る表現。
● Expression with
monotones and
shades of brown.

カラフル
Colorful

モダン
Modern

リアリズム
Realism

クラシック
（ネオクラシズム）
Classic
(neo-classisism)

凡例
（データの読み方）

LEGEND
(A Guide to How to Read Data)

タイトル： **a**：Title

デザイナー： **b**：Designer

クライアント： **c**：Client

コメント： **d**：Comment

Step-by-Step
Architectural Marker Techniques

Copyright ©1991 Graphic-sha Publishing Co., Ltd.

1-9-12 Kudankita, Chiyoda-ku, Tokyo 102, Japan

ISBN4-7661-0638-5

Printed in Japan

First Printing, May 1991

第 一 章
色彩と雰囲気を中心にした
イメージ・コンセプトスケッチ

Color Application and Expression
of the Atmosphere of Subjects.

Chapter 1

❶
水性サインペンでの墨入れ完了の状態。
ボードの鉛筆の下書きは、鉛筆の線が見えなくなるまで、
しっかりと消す。以外のプロセスでもすべて同じ。
❷
パントーンマーカーの淡い色調（パステルトーン）から描く。
このパースのイメージとして、全体にやわらかな
パステルトーンの空気のような、
また空間のような感じを出すため、
淡い色調を全体の空間の色気を出すように、
マーカーの流れを、まず色調の弱い、
ブルー系とグリーン系のマーカーで全体にやわらかく描く。
その際、光、スポットライト、明暗、
形の流れなどを意識しながら、繊細に描く。
マーカーを使用するときはもたもたせずに、いっきに描く。
マーカーの線を走らせながら、途中で止めないこと。
直線も曲線も、そして一番難しい自由曲線も、
自信をもって描く。あとは慣れで
その人のタッチは千差万別、個性で描くこと。

❸
この段階では、寒色系のパステルトーンで
両面のニュアンスを作ってみたが、
次の段階として暖色系の色を入れる。
画面の色のポイントを作るのである。
イスやテーブル、鳥や花、惑星、建物などに色を入れる。
一つ気をつけることは、黄色系をあまり入れすぎると
他の色より黄色だけが飛んでしまうので気をつける。
この画面の中での寒色系と暖色系の色の配色は、
7：3ぐらいの感じにすると画面の雰囲気がちょうどいい。
❹
こまかなニュアンスを入れる段階だが、
基本的にどこにどの色を入れるというのは、
このパースの場合はほとんど決まっていない。
ただ、まず画面中央の花の形をしたソファー席は、
はなやかな色で表現したいし、
海へ流れる川、そして空間をつつむ花や植物、
鳥たちにも色のリズムをつけたい。
ステージで踊る人物にもスポットの光の流れを作りたい。

空の色もパンチをもたせたいので、ブルーを濃くする。
全体のトーンに幅をもたせるためにバイオレット、
グリーン、ブルー系のチントマーカーを使用し、
トーンのバリエーションを増やす。
またそれらのトーンの重なり合いの上より画面の中で、
カラーブレンドマーカーを上からなぞると、
今までのマーカーの色が画面の中で水彩絵具のように
やわらかなトーンになる。
それでも描き出せないこまかなニュアンスは、
やわらかな色鉛筆を使いやさしいタッチで描きこむ。
植物の葉はグリーン、花や鳥、
そしてソファー席にも色を入れる。
さらに画面に深みをもたせるために、暗いところや
影のところを部分的に濃いマーカーでタッチを入れる。
黒キャップのパントーンマーカーは細いタッチの
マーカーなので、最後のこまかな描きこみに便利である。
全体に描き込みができたら、
最後に版下用ポスターカラー、ホワイトで
明るいアクセントにタッチを入れる。

このスケッチは、全体が楽園をイメージさせる光や色彩にあふれ、
一つ一つの物の質感よりも全体の空気や色の流れのようなイメージが、
重要な表現のポイントになる。
そのために、マーカーのテクニックも空間の中、画面の中で心地よい
色彩の流れが、まさにエスニック音楽のように感じられるようにしたい。
使うマーカーの種類はモノトーンのグレー系は避け、

光や明暗も色味のあるマーカーで表現していく。
マーカーのテクニックは、ダイレクトに描く普通の単純なテクニックでいい。
途中でチントマーカーにより色のトーンに幅をもたせ、
カラーブレンドによりニュアンスもつける。
まずは描く本人が楽園の音楽でも聞きながら気分に浸り、
その表現のダイレクトな描き方を考えることが重要である。

Project 1

オープンパフォーミングスペース
ディスコ＆レストランバー オアシスのイメージ

Open performance space
Discoteques, restaurant bars ; an image of oasis.

This sketch should be filled with light and color in order to create an image of paradise within the entire picture. The creation of a colorful flowing image is therefore more important to the complete effect than the individual quality of the elements. To achieve this, one will need a certain degree of marker technique to produce a pleasant color flow within the space in the same style as a piece of ethnic music. Naturally, grey tones or monotones should not be used here; color markers should be used to express even the light and shade. One should draw directly with an confident and simple technique. Change to tint markers half way through in order to add some depth to the tones and work in subtle nuances by blending the colors. It is important for the artist to steep him or herself in a merry atmosphere by listening to some background music that conjours up the feeling of paradise as this will help with the direct thought process to enable good expression.

使 用 マ ー カ ー
Markers used in the drawing.

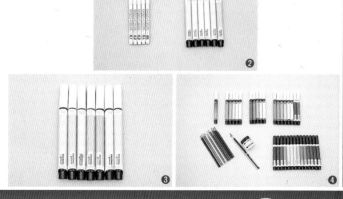

❶
No markers were used.
❷
Pantone 290-M
Pantone 304-M
Pantone 317-M
Pantone 365-M
Pantone 351-M
Pantone 250-M
❸
Pantone 475-M
Pantone 162-M
Pantone 489-M
Pantone 182-M
Pantone 176-M
Pantone 100-M
Pantone 459-M

Pantone 347 tint 10%-80%
Pantone violet tint 10%-80%
Pantone process cyan tint 10%-100%
❹
Pantone 300-M

Pantone process blue-M

Fine markers
Pantone 144-F
Pantone orange 021-F
Pantone 485-F
Pantone rhodamine red-F
Pantone purple-F
Pantone 259-F
Pantone reflex blue-F
Pantone blue 072-F
Pantone 300-F
Pantone 347-F
Pantone 375-F
Pantone 395-F
Pantone yellow-F
Pantone 116-F

Color grade markers
Soft-color pencils
White poster color for block-copy use
2 or 3 brushes to draw in features

この際も単に白を塗るのではなく、白を入れて、
また一段階画面が新鮮になるように、
いろいろなニュアンスで明るいところにタッチをつける。
一応これで完成となるが、でき上がりを見て、
画面の中より鳥のさえずりや、水の流れ、
遠くの海の波の音、花の薫り、人々の楽しさが感じられ、
楽園の音楽が聞こえるような気がしたら、
このパースは完成ということになる。

❶
The inking with a water-color felt-tip pen has been completed. The rough pencil sketch should be erased until all lines have completely disappeared from the board. This will apply to all other processes.

❷
Commence the drawing in the lighter shades of panton colors (pastel tones). In order to create a soft pastel tone expression similar to the image of a perspective drawing, use blue and green tone markers with a soft touch to draw in the light-tone sections and the flow of the markers that add some color to the space.

At the same time, the detail should be drawn in with an awareness of the lights, spot-lights, light and shade and the actual flow of the shapes.

All marker strokes should be bold and without hesitation. Once the line has been started, do not stop the progress of the marker. The straight and curved lines and the most difficult free-hand curves must be drawn with full confidence. Experience in this will create an individual drawing style. Individuality should always be shown in a drawing.

❸
At this stage, cold color pastel tones have been used to add some nuance to the picture. The next stage is to add some warm colors in order to produce the color points in the picture. One point to remember is that yellow shades should not be overused as they have a tendency to stand out more than other colors. A ratio of seven to three of cold colors and warm colors will add the appropriate atmosphere to this picture.

❹
This is the stage in which detail is added to the picture, but in the case of perspective drawing it is unlikely that the color positions have been fixed. Initially, however, I would like to express the flower-shaped sofa in the center of the picture in a bright color and then add some rhythm to the color scheme of the river flowing to the sea, the flowers, plants and the birds which surround the space. Furthermore, I intend to add the beam of a spot-light shining on the person standing on stage. The blue of the sky has been darkened to put more punch to the sky section, and the tone variations have been increased by the use of violet, green and blue tint markers in order to give a wider range to the entire tone. If one traces the color-blend markers over the above tones, the colors will blend and produce soft tones similar to water color paints. Should any nuances that cannot be produced in detail appear, these can be depicted with soft color pencils using a gentle touch. Color in the leaves of the plants in green, and add some color to the flowers, birds and sofa.

Use darker markers to touch-up the dark or shadowy sections in order to produce a sense of depth. The black-capped pantone marker is handy for adding the final details owing to its slender point. Once the entire picture has been drawn in, the next stage is to add the light accents by using white poster color for block-copy use as a final touch. During this process, one should try to add the white to the lighter parts of the picture whilst studying the various nuances to improve the freshness of the picture and prevent it from seeming to have just been drawn. The work is now by-and-large finished. If you can hear the birds chirping, the water murmmuring, the waves splashing and smell the flowers and feel the happy spirit of the people just by staring into the picture, then I would say that the perspective has been completed with good marks.

プロセス
Process

カラーウェイ
Color Way

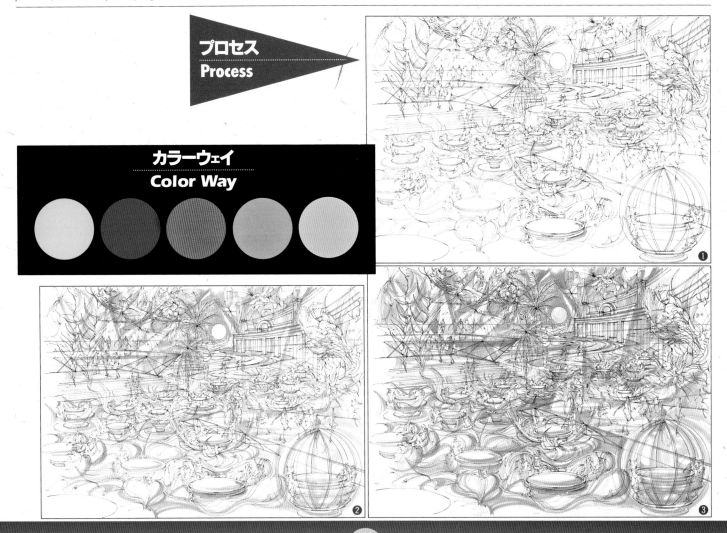

★
チントマーカー＆カラーブレンド
Tint marker and Color blend

マーカーを使用している時に一番気になるところが色と色とが重なるエッジの部分。もちろんこのエッジをうまく利用することがマーカーをうまく使いこなすコツともいえる。しかし，どうしても滑らかな面を表現したいときがある。こんな要望に応えたのが，チントマーカーとカラーブレンドである。この2種類のマーカーの特色は，色のグラデーションとカラートーンのスムーズな流れの面を表現するために開発されたもの。

使い方はいたって簡単。チントマーカーの色濃度は，10％，20％，40％，60％，80％，100％の6段階で用意されている。これを，必要な幅だけ段階的に塗り分ける。このときはまだエッジが重なって見えている。その重なったエッジの上からカラーブレンドで軽くこするようにする。これだけで，重なった部分のエッジが消え，境目にきれいなカラートーンができ，全面になだらかなグラデーションが仕上がる。

The thing which requires the most concentration when using markers is the overlapping edges between colors. Of course, once one has learnt to take good advantage of these edges, it could be said that the user has commandeered the use of markers. However, there are times when one wishes to express a feeling of the colors flowing into each other. To respond to such requests are tinted markers and color blends. These two types of markers were especially developed to enable the expression of smooth and flowing colors, gradation and color tones.

The use of these markers is extremely simple. There are six different levels of color depth available in the tinted marker range : 10％, 20％, 40％, 60％, 80％ and 100％. These can be layered on to meet any required width. At this point the edges will be overlapped. The color bledd is then applied lightly over the overlapping areas. This will erase the overlapping edges and create a beautiful color tone on the borders and a smooth gradation will be produced.

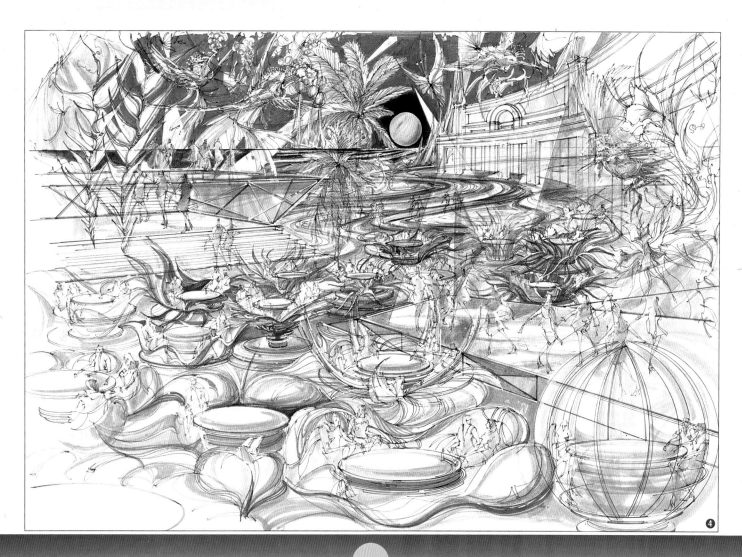

❹

❶
水性サインペンでの墨入れ完了の状態。
ボードの鉛筆の下書きは, 鉛筆の線が見えなくなるまで,
しっかりと消す。以外のプロセスでもすべて同じ。
❷
まず, 薄いブルー系で画面に全体的にタッチを入れる。
このパースが, 前出のオアシスのパースと違うのは,
モダニズム風の色面の構成なので色彩の分別のラインが
硬質な直線や曲線でできていること。
しいていえば, 点景に自由曲線が入っているくらいである。
したがって, マーカーのタッチも硬質なタッチで
描くべきである。
硬質で, ピリッとしたタッチで全体のラインにそって,
画面にニュアンスをつける。
明暗のニュアンスも意識してみる。
❸
プロセス❷のように, 淡いグリーン系を入れる。
❹❺
画面に深さと色のニュアンスをつける段階。
チントマーカーの重ねとブレンドマーカーにより
画面にニュアンスをあたえながら,
ブルー, バイオレット, グリーン, イエローの色のを出す。

❻❼❽
プロセス❺の段階までで空間全体の
色の流れを表現したが,
この段階から空間の深さと硬質性を表現したい。
まず, 各色の彩度の高い色をポイントに表現する。
洋服と空間全体のバランスを見て彩色する。
パーテーションの透明感の表現に気をつける。
色鉛筆もまぜ合わせながら, 空間にしまりをあたえる。
線と線, 面と面とのエッジに明暗, 寒暖, 色相, 彩度などの
ニュアンスと, パンチをあたえる。
これで空間が生き生きとしてくる。
イメージとして最終的に深みがあり, 重さもあり,
色の響きあいによるある種の艶のようなものを表現したい。
この空間に入ったとたんに, 洋服の色気が空間全体から
感じられるように表現したいのである。
おのおのの質感より, 色の深さ, 響きあいの
マーカーの表現をめざすのである。
手前のステップおよびパンチのある空間との対比を表現し,
中央の空間を強調する。

❶
The inking with a water-color felt-tip pen has

been completed. The rough pencil sketch
should be erased until all lines have
completely disappeared from the board.
This will apply to all other processes.
❷
First of all, add a few rough touches with a
light-blue marker to the entire drawing.
The thing that makes this picture different
from the previous drawing of an oasis is the
lines that devide the colors. Hard straight and
curved lines are used here as the drawing
has been composed in a modernistic style
and color design. If anything, only the human
figures will be needed to be drawn by hand.
Hand-touch marker techniques will be
required for this. Add a sharp touch along the
entire line to add some nuance to the
picture. Try to include the shading nuances
as well.
❸
Add a light green tone to the picture in the
same way as in process #2.
❹❺
This is the stage in which depth and color

このブティックは, まず最終的に, 色のトーンが空間全体を
表現されるために, 淡いトーンから濃いトーン, 軽いトーンから
重たくて渋いトーンまで, そうとうの色の幅が必要とされる。
そのためにはマーカーの色を何度も塗り重ね,

いろいろのマーカーのトーンのバリエーションを作りながら,
空間の中の色の響きあいを作る。
色が一番重要なポイントとなるデザインだからである。

Project 2 モダニティー・ファッションブティックM
Modernity Fashion Boutique M.

A wide range of colors such as light, dark, heavy and
sober tones will eventually be required to express the
entire space of this boutique. It is therefore necessary to
produce effective color tones within the space by adding
many coats of various color markers to the picture in
order to produce the correct tones of color.
Remember that the most important design point of a
drawing is the color.

使 用 マ ー カ ー
Markers used in the drawing.

❶
No markers used.
❷
Pantone 290-M
Pantone 304-M
Pantone 317-M
❸
Pantone 351-M
Pantone 365-M
Pantone tint 347 10%-40%
❹❺
Color grade.
Pantone 100-M
Pantone 162-M
Pantone 176-M
Pantone 182-M
Pantone 250-M
Pantone 459-M
Pantone 475-M
Pantone 489-M
Pantone 548-M

Tint markers.
Pantone violet 10%-40%
Pantone process cyan 10%-100%
Pantone 375 10%-40%
Pantone process yellow 10%-60%
❻❼❽
Pantone violet 10%-100%
Pantone process cyan 10%-100%

Pantone 375 10%-40%
Pantone 347 10%-80%

Color grade.
10 color pencils.
Features, etc.
Pantone 370-M
Pantone 374-M
Pantone reflex blue-M
Pantone 300-M
Pantone process blue-M
Pantone 140-M
Pantone 259-M
Pantone 103-M
Pantone 110-M
Pantone 163-M
Pantone 116-F
Pantone 114-F
Pantone 021-F
Pantone 485-F
Pantone rhodamine red-F
Pantone purple-F
Pantone 259-F
Pantone blue-F
Pantone reflex blue-F
Pantone 300-F
Pantone 347-F
Pantone 375-F
Pantone 396-F
Pantone yellow-F

nuance is added to the picture. While adding the nuance touches by over-coating the tint markers and blend markers try to produce a feeling of depth with the blue-violet, green and yellow colors.

❻❼❽

Up until process # 5, the color flows of the entire space has been expressed, and now I would like to use this stage to express the depth and hardeness of the space.

Firstly, use high-chroma colors in each tone. Consider the balance between the costumes and the entire space before commencing the coloring. Take extra care over the expression of the transparent appearence of the partition. Use color pencils to add firmness to the picture. Add some shading to the edges between the lines and create nuances by the use of cold and dark hues and chromas in order to add punch to the drawing.

This will bring the space more alive.

Eventually I would like to produce a picture that has depth, weight and a kind of gloss created by the effect of the colors.

Once we have reached this stage, it is necessary to give ones full attention to the coloring of the clothes. I intend to concentrate on expressing the depth of the colors and marker effects rather than the individual qualities. I have left the light colors of the steps and the human figures in the foreground as they are purposely in order to emphasize the center space by expressing the contrast with vigour.

技法ワンポイント
One point technique

★
パントンカラーマーカー
Pantone color marker

パントンカラーマーカーは200色を越える幅の広いカラーをもつマーカー。ペン先は白いキャップの太書き，黒いキャップの細書き，グレーのキャップの極細書きの3種類。油性のため乾燥が早く，太書きと細書きを重ね合わせてもにじます，発色性の良さは定評のあるところ。ただし，油性であるがためコピー用紙やファクシミリ用紙に使用すると，線がにじんでしまうことがあるので注意したい。

Panton color marker range extend to over 200 different colors. There are three types of points : the white cap is for thick drawing, the black cap for slender drawing, and the grey cap of extra fine drawing. Being oil based, they dry quickly, the thick and fine points may be used together without the fear of blurring, and they have a reputation for good coloring. However, note should be taken that their oil base will cause blurring the line on photocopy paper and facsimile paper.

プロセス
Process

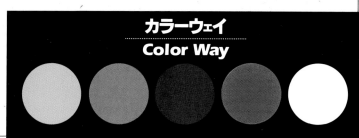

カラーウェイ
Color Way

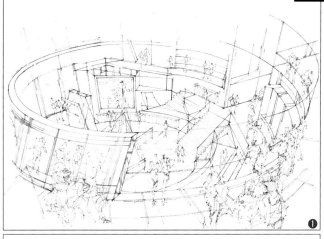

❶

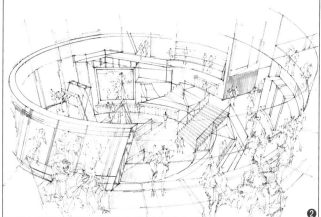

❷

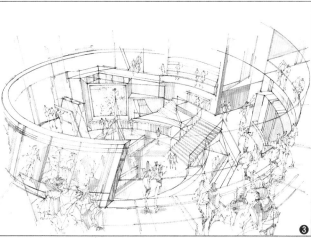

❸

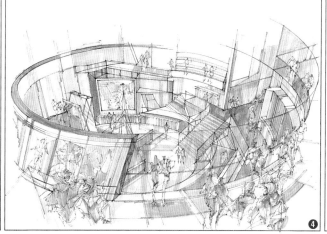

❹

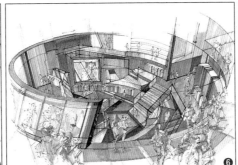

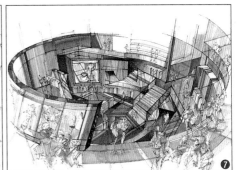

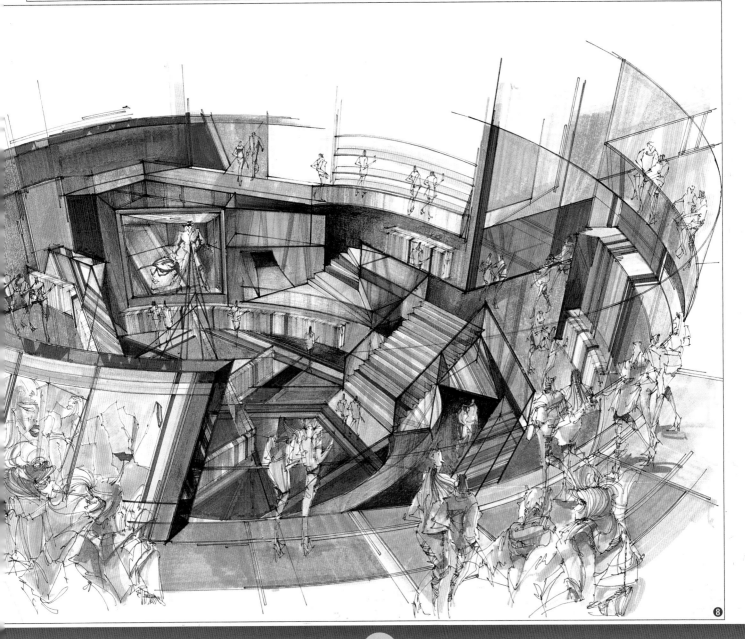

ファッション・ストリート レインボー・イメージ：a：FASHON STREET-RAINBOW IMAGE
エアー・スタジオ：b：Air Studio
このスケッチのような表現は，：d：Expression such as that apparent in this sketch
ある意味でこれからのパースの可能性の一つであると思う。 somehow has in its hands the future of perspectives.
ファッショナブルなストリートとカラフルな色彩。 The fashionable street and the colorful artwork.
ファッションショーから抜け出たような人々の一瞬の動き。 The momentary movements of the people who look as
それらの空気感の表現を，回りくどい説明でなく if they have just stepped out of a fashion show.
全体のダイレクト・イメージとしてとらえたスケッチである。 This sketch has captured the expression
of the sensatios available in the air
through the method of direct image, not as commentary.

コカ・コーラ イメージサイン：a：COCA COLA-IMAGE SIGN
エアー・スタジオ：b：Air Studio
画面の中にサイケデリックでカラフルな色彩のトーンをどのようなバランスで入れるかが重要。：d：What balance of psychedelic and colorful tonse should be filling this picture？
中間色をさけ，画面の軽快感を作りたい。　Avoid using natural colors.
色彩のリズム感や色面の構成，面積の大小，タッチの飛ばし方，　we need to produce a feeling of jauntiness in the picture.
ニュアンスなどもこの画面のポイント。　A rhythmical sense of colors should be used to
compose the color face.
The total are, the way in which the color is
splashed over the page and the creation of nuances
are counted as the main points of this picture.

ブティック パープルレイン：a：BUTIQE-PURPLE RAIN
エアー・スタジオ：b：Air Studio

Ｚ ゾーン トータル・イベント・スペース：a：Z-ZONE-TOTAL EVENT SPACE
エアー・スタジオ：b：Air Studio
ロシア風な建築のイメージのパターン。：d：An image pattern of Russian-style architecture.
色彩は強烈な赤とグリーンでハレーションを　　A contrast of complimentary colors that will be
おこすくらいのきわどい補色の対比が狙い。　strong enough to produce a halation of bright reds and greens.
強引に強い赤と緑を画面に塗り込む。　Forcefully color the picture with strong reds and greens,
その中に色彩のハーモニーを作りたい。　and the harmony of color will be naturally produced within.

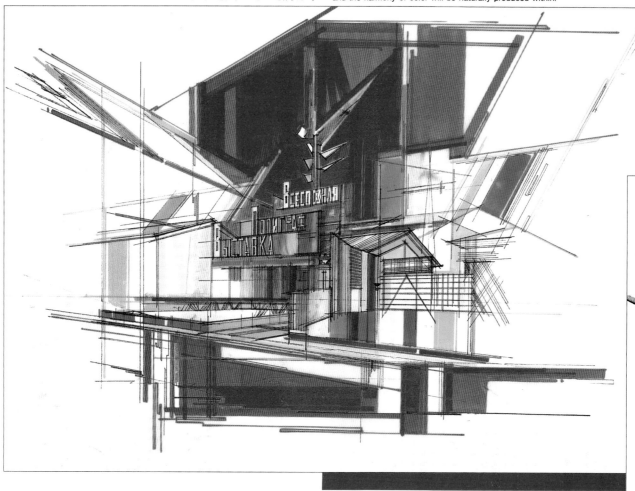

パフォーミング・ビル　ビッグ・バーン：a：PAFORMING BUILDING-BIG BANG
エアー・スタジオ：b：Air Studio
劇場，ディスコなど，多目的なパフォーマンス・スペースを：d：This is the facade design of a building designed
必要とするビルのファサード・デザインである。　　　for various and multi-purpose performances
イメージスケッチなので，あえてあまり説明的には表現せず，　such as stagework, theatr and discoteque, etc.
派手な色彩を回りの空間も含めて配置する。　　Being an image sketch, bright colors have been
色彩を重視したイメージによるスケッチである。　deliberately arranged in the space and surroundings
to avoid using a commentary style expression.
This is a sketch image fo a color-image.

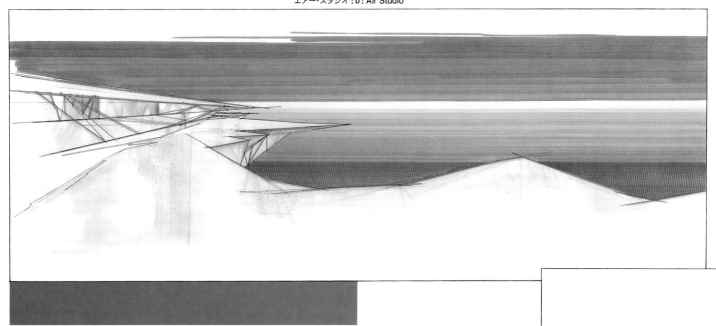

シンボリック・タワー：a：SYMBOLIC TOWER

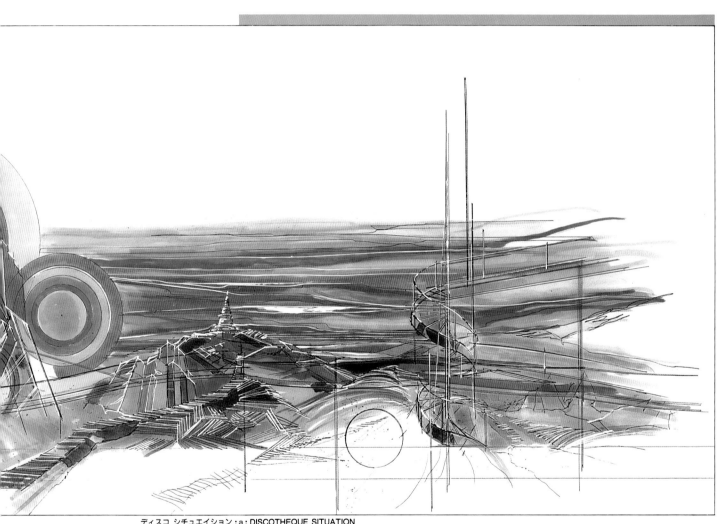

ディスコ シチュエイション：a：DISCOTHEQUE SITUATION
エアー・スタジオ：b：Air Studio

仏料理店 赤い部屋：a：FRENCH RESTAURANT-RED ROOM
アース・ファクトリー：b：Earth Factory

ファッションビル&ストリート レインボー：a：FASHON BUILDING & STREET-RAINBOW
エアー・スタジオ：b：Air Studio
ラフなイメージスケッチ。このスケッチは動き，：d：This sketch has more complicated movement, coloring,
空間，形などがより複雑に表現されている。　space and shapes than in the other rough image sketches. .
色彩の流れはさらに複雑に表現され，　The deeper expression of the colors flowing
かなり複雑な画面構成で細長い画面に　throughout the picture and the detailed composition
空間の奥行と臨場感をあたえている。　of the content adds a depth of space
今まであまり見ないスタイルのスケッチだが，　and presence to the long surface of the work.
これからの時代ますます必要とされる表現と思われる。　This style of expressing sketches has not been
very popular until recently,
but it is expected to take off in the future.

スペース 彼女の夢：a：SPACE-DREAMING OF HER
エアー・スタジオ：b：Air Studio
一人の女が未だ見ぬ世界を見たいと思い，世界へのイメージをかきたてる。:d: A woman wishes to see a part of the world
心の中のイメージ表現がテーマである。　that she has never seen before and draws an image of it.
パースペクティブな，より抽象的に世界中のモチーフと　The image in her mind is an expression of the space of theme.
ファッショナブルな女のイメージが対比され，　The motif of the world and the image of the
構図はマックス・エルンストの幻想的風景画風となる。　fashionable woman have been contrasted more abstractly
色彩は紫を中心としたトーンの流れでシックな雰囲気を盛り上げる。　than in a perspective drawing and is composed
イメージの抽象的アイデア・スケッチである。　in the style of Max Ernst's fantastic landscape painting.
The tones of purple as the main color increases
the chic atmosphere. It is a sketch of an idea image.

JR 信濃町プロジェクト : a : JR SHINANOMACHI PROJECT
株式会社リンク，三原実 : b : Link Co.,Ltd., Minoru Mihara
株式会社リンク : c : Link Co.,Ltd.
信濃町プロジェクトの一番強い色彩のパターン。 : d : The strongest color pattern included in the Shinano-machi project.
香港の九龍城のような縦横無尽に空間を走る回廊。 The hall runs in all directions throughout
ネオン管のサイン。テント，超ド派手な色彩。 the space like a Kowloon castle.
その中をうごめく無国籍な人々。 Neon tube signs, tents, super bright colors and
これらの空間の中を動き回る空気感を， hordes of wriggling people with the same nationality throughout.
派手な色彩と飛ぶようなタッチで画面に躍動感を表現する。 The sensation drifting through the air
is expressed by using extremely bright colors
splashed on to produce a sense of livliness.

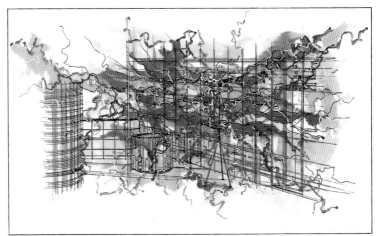

ディスコ&レーザー スペース・イメージ：a：DISCOTHEQUE & LASER-SPACE IMAGE
エアー・スタジオ：b：Air Studio

JR 信濃町プロジェクト：a：JR SHINANOMACHI PROJECT
株式会社リンク、三原実：b：Link Co.,Ltd., Minoru Mihara
株式会社リンク：c：Link Co.,Ltd.
信濃町プロジェクトの一つ。全体に木調で構成。：d：The Shinano-machi project.
色彩は茶系と空のブルーの対比のみ。　　　The entire picture is composed of wood.
すっきりとした表現をしている。　　　　　The only colors within the picture are shades of brown
　　　　　　　　　　　　　　　　　　　and the blue of the sky. It is very neatly expressed.

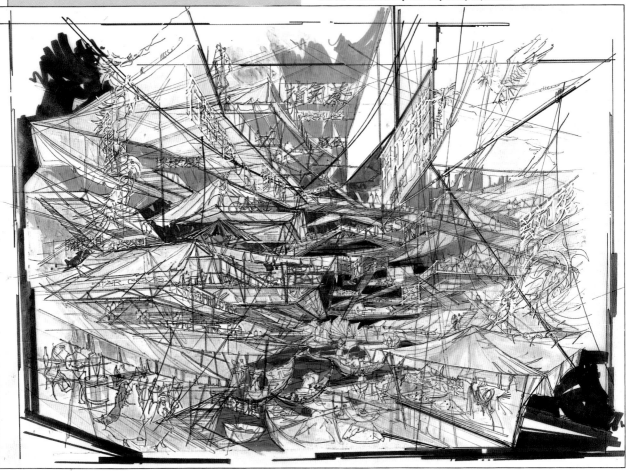

JR 信濃町プロジェクト ：a：JR SHINANO-MACHI PROJECT
株式会社リンク，三原実 ：b：Link Co.,Ltd., Minoru Mihara
株式会社リンク ：c：Link Co.,Ltd.
信濃町プロジェクトの少しトーンがやわらかくなったパターン。：d：A version of the Shinanao-machi project in lighter tones.
ややパステルトーンで空気を表現するように、　　A small amount of pastel tones have been lightly
やわらかめに入れる。　　added to the sketch to express the existence of air.

ファッション・ビル プライム : a : FASHION BUILDING-PRIME
エアー・ファクトリー : b : Air Factory

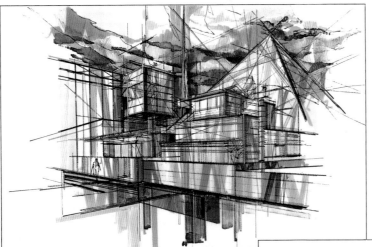

ギャラリー&ファッション・ビル : a : GARERY & FASHION BUILDING
アース・ファクトリー : b : Earth Factory

エスニック・レストラン 花の楽園：a：ETHNIC RESTAURANT-PARADISE OF FLOWER
エアー・スタジオ：b：Air Studio
南国の空間を強烈な色彩の対比で表現する：d：This is also a paradise-style image sketch.
楽園風イメージスケッチ。　　　The southern country style space has been expressed
画面全体が強烈な色彩により空気が染ってしまうようだ。　by the contrast of deep colors, which give off an image
無国籍風でエスニックな音楽が聞えてきそうな感覚を　that the entire sketch has been steeped in strong colors.
荒々しいタッチと色彩で表現した。　The feeling of non-nationality
and the unique music-like image has been expressed
with rough touches and color marker techniques.

山本寛斉パフォーミング・スペース：a：YAMAMOTO KANSAI PAFORMING SPACE
山本寛斉，エアー・スタジオ：b：Yamamoto Kansai, Air Studio
株式会社山本寛斉：c：Yamamoto Kansai Co.,Ltd.

サンリオ・ショップ イメージスケッチ：a：SANRIO SHOP-IMAGE SKETCH
サンリオ：c：Sanrio Co.,Ltd.

風と水の建築：a：ARCHITECTURE OF WIND & WATER
エアー・スタジオ：b：Air Studio
流れるような水と空気の中に建つ建築のイメージを：d：The title of this sketch is The Building Amongst Wind and Water
パステルトーンの中のブルーを中心に、　　　　　and the image of the building actually seeming
マーカーの色の流れによって　　　　　　　to be part of the flow of the wind and water
建築と空気と水の一体感を表現した。　　　　has been produced by expressing
the its oneness building with the air and water
by the method of the marker color flow technique
using colors based on blues and pastel tones.

ディスコ オアシス :a: DISCOTHEQUE-OASIS
エアー・スタジオ :b: Air Studio
一般の透視点が消失したこのイメージスケッチは、:d: An image sketch of a discoteque Oasis.
透視点が消えた画面の中を鳥や植物や蝶が自由に乱舞する。 This sketch has lost its general perspective points.
水晶体風な透明なイメージと虹のような円を描く光りは、 The birds, plants and butterflies are freely and boisterously dancing
ブルーを中心としたやわらかなパステルトーンで表現した。 in the picture without the restraints of perspective.
その中に色のポイントとなる The crystal-look transparent image
オレンジや赤の鳥や蝶を乱舞させた。 and the light drawing a rainbow-like semi-circle have been
楽園風のイメージスケッチである。 expressed in soft pastel tone markers based around blue.
Amongst this the orange and red birds and butterflies
have been arranged to fly around rowdily as color points.
This is a paradise-stlye image sketch.

体験ゾーン R : a : EXPERIENCE ZONE R

ディスコ&ディスコホール中央 オブジェ：**a**：DISCOTHEQUE & CENTER OF HALL, OBJET
エアー・スタジオ：**b**：Air Studio

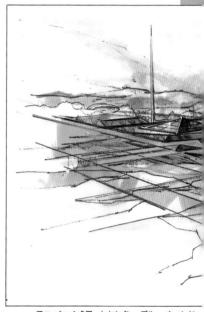

ファッション&アートセンター ブルー・ウィンド：
アース・ファクトリー：

レストラン ナチュラルハウス：a：RESTAURANT-NATURAL HOUSE

a：FASHION & ART CENTER-BLUE WIND
b：Earth Factory

レストラン・ビル：a：RESTAURANT BUILDING

バーラー・イーグル 喫茶&ゲームコーナー：**a**：PARLOR EAGLE-TEAROOM & GAME CORNER
エアー・スタジオ：**b**：Air Studio
イーグル：**c**：Eagle Co.,Ltd.

バーラー・イーグル 喫茶&ゲームコーナー：**a**：PARLOR EAGLE-TEAROOM & GAME CORNER
エアー・スタジオ：**b**：Air Studio
イーグル：**c**：Eagle Co.,Ltd.

バーラー・イーグル：**a**：PARLOR EAGLE
エアー・スタジオ：**b**：Air Studio
イーグル：**c**：Eagle Co.,Ltd.

サントリー・バー イメージスケッチ：a：SUNTORY BAR-IMAGE SKETCH
サン・アド，エアー・スタジオ：b：Sun AD Co.,Ltd., Air Studio

パーラー・イーグル ファサード：a：PARLOR EAGLE-FACARDE
エアー・スタジオ：b：Air Studio
イーグル：c：Eagle Co.,Ltd.

ホテル V&V ラウンジ&バー：a：HOTEL V&V-LOUNGE & BAR
エアー・スタジオ：b：Air Studio

Zゾーン トータル・イベント・スペース：a：Z-ZONE-TOTAL EVENT SPACE
エアー・スタジオ：b：Air Studio

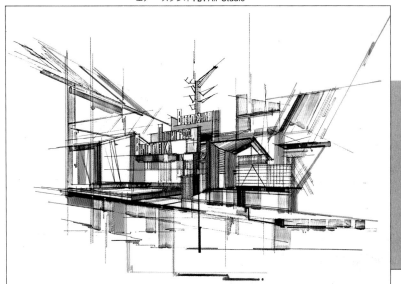

コカコーラ イメージサイン：a：COCACOLA-IMAGE SIGN

第二章
空間と形態を中心にした
イメージ・コンセプトスケッチ
The Expression of Space,
Perspective, and Form.
Chapter 2

❶
ボードに鉛筆の下書きをする。このスケッチの場合，
人物による点景が重要なポイントになる。
まず，点景をすべて描き込む。
点景により，建物までの距離感，スケール感，
空間の雰囲気，ファッション，風俗感など，
いろいろな建物のまわりの空気感を表現する。
人物のファッション，ヘアースタイル，
これからビルに入ろうとする人々の期待感，ざわめき，
語らい，動き，色，人々の視線の方向などを表現する。
人間や車など点景を表現するとき，一番重要なポイントは，
タッチ，1本1本の線を同じスピードで描かないこと。
これにつきる。同一のスピードで描くと，
せっかくの空間の躍動感が表現できない。
まず，1本1本の線に，スピード感の違いと，
リズムをあたえることが重要である。

1本の線にリズムと表情，生気をあたえること。
これが，結局はすべてのプロセスにいえることであり，
しいては，パースに生気をあたえ，
見る人に何かを感じさせることができる。
❷
墨入れ完成。
❸
グレー系の非常に薄いトーンで，全体に水墨画を描くように，
あるいは空気遠近法のように，やわらかなハイトーンの
グレーによる空気と，明暗のトーンの流れを軽くのせる。
このデザインはハイテックなデザインなので，
グレーは冷たいクールグレーで描き込む。
タッチはペンの線にそって直線的に描いたり，
ラフにフリーハンドでマーカーのタッチをかたまりとして，
ざくっという感じで描いたりする。
そう，ざっくりという感じである。

明るいところに適当な白を残しながら描く。
あくまでも単調にならないように，
タッチにもスピード感の違いと表情のニュアンスをつける。
❹
クールグレーの中間のトーンで描き進む。
この段階では全体の空間の違いや質感，
たとえば，ガラスの光った感じや
ステンレスバーの金属感などを描き込む。
ステンレスのバーの金属感の映り込みは，サインペンで直接
ギラッと表現する。これもポイントである。
中央のファサードの建築を明るめに残す。
❺
プロセス❹の段階の上に，濃いグレーで建築物のまわり，
アウトラインなどに明暗のリズムをあたえ表情を作る。
プロセス❹の上にもう一度濃いタッチを慎重にあたえる。
慎重，なおかつリズミカルに，アクセントを描き完成となる。

このスケッチは，ケントボードにモノトーンで濃淡および立体感，
イメージを表現し，これでまず，モノトーンのパースを完成させる。
それで第2原図（トレーシングペーパーにコピー）を数枚取り，
この建築のデザインの色彩と質感のバリエーションを
何パターンか表現し，それらの中から，
デザインの可能性をさぐるという作業である。
第2原図へのマーカー着彩は，ボードとは違って，
トレーシングペーパーの裏側から着彩し描き込む。

最終段階に入ったところで，裏と表に，
同時に描き込み，完成させるという方法である。
これをケントボードやスチレンボードに張って
提出するわけだが，この方法はむしろ，
直接ボードに描くよりも，マーカーの発色がよく表現されるし，
何より何パターンも描け，
失敗しても原画よりコピーして何枚も描けるという利点がある。
この方法は初心者やプロに幅広くお勧めしたい。

Project 3

トータル ファッションビル
ファサード 計画案プロセス

Total Fashion Building

Facade Planning and the Process.

This sketch has been drawn on Kentboard and expresses the light, shade, cubic shapes and images in monotones. This monotone perspective is complete for the time being. Now we go onto the second original drawing. I took several copies of the original drawing (using tracing paper) in order to create as many various patterns of the design as possible by changing the colors and quality appearences of each picture.
For the coloring in this second original drawing, I used the method of coloring from the back of the tracing paper; a different method from that used on the board.

The colors will be put into place simultaneously from the back and the front at the final stage to complete the picture. This will then be stuck onto the Kentboard or styrene-board for submitting. This method can be recommended to a wide range of people from beginners to professionals as the colors of the markers will come out much clearer than if added directly onto the board. Most of all, this method has the added advantage of allowing one to draw many different patterns and take as many copies of the original as one feels necessary.

使 用 マーカー
Markers used in the drawing.

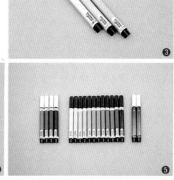

❶	Extra black-M
No markers were used.	Color blend
❷	Color blend
No markers were used.	
❸	Fine points.
Cool grey 1-M	Cool grey 1-F
Cool grey 2-M	Cool grey 2-F
Cool grey 3-M	Cool grey 3-F
❹	Cool grey 4-F
Cool grey 4-M	Cool grey 5-F
Cool grey 5-M	Cool grey 6-F
Cool grey 6-M	Cool grey 7-F
Cool grey 7-M	Cool grey 8-F
Cool grey 8-M	Cool grey 9-F
❺	Cool grey 10-F
Cool grey 9-M	Cool grey 11-F
Cool grey 10-M	Extra black-F
Cool grey 11-M	

First draw a rough sketch on the board with a pencil. Next add all of the human figures roughly. Humans play an important part in this sketch as they are used to express the various surroundings of the building such as distance, scale, atmosphere, fashion and customs. One should take care to express well the fashions, hairstyles - as these will on reflect the type of people expected to enter the shop - the ripple of talk and laughter, movement, color and the direction of their eyes. When drawing in the human forms, it is important to ensure that all of the figures are drawn with the different touches and speeds. This is the best way to express the images correctly. The special feel of lively motion will be lost if everything is drawn with the same touch. Each line must be given a sense of rhythm, expression and life. This will apply to all processes and, after all, will help produce a perspective drawing that will be full of life and impress its viewers.

The inking complete.

Using a very light grey tone, spread the color over the entire space as if one is drawing an Indian ink or air painting. Then add the air, light and dark tones and allow them to flow through the picture by using a soft high tone grey. Use a cool grey to draw with, as this is a high-tech design. Various touches can then be added to the picture. One can draw along the pen lines with a lineal touch,
draw roughly in freehand, or, one can add a touch of marker in a mass block. While drawing,
be sure to leave some white in the light areas. Use different speeds in the application and add some subtle nuances in order to avoid a feeling of monotony.

❹
Use a neutral tone of cool grey to further the painting. In this stage the distinction and qualities of the actual space should be drawn; the shiny effects of the glass and the metalic effect of the stainless steel bar, for example. Use a felt-tip pen to express the reflection of the stainless steel bar by drawing a flash directly onto it.
Another important point to note is that it is necessary to leave the facade in the center in a lighter color.

❺
Add some rhythmic light and shading to the surroundings and outline of the building over the process made in #4 with a dark grey marker to create expression. Then add some darker touches to process #4. Draw in the accents carefully and rhythmically to complete.

プロセス
Process

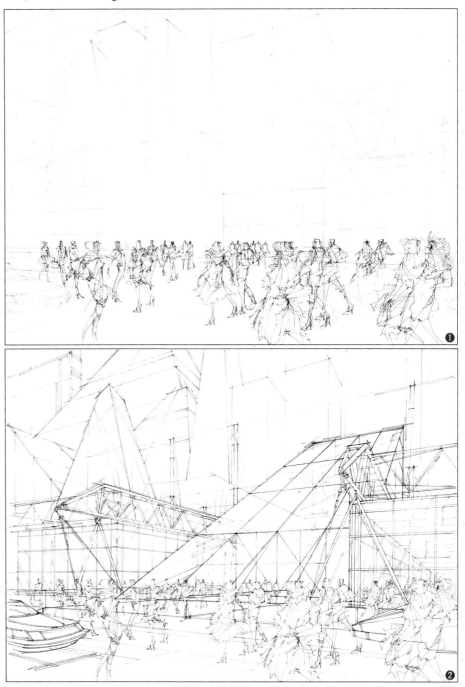

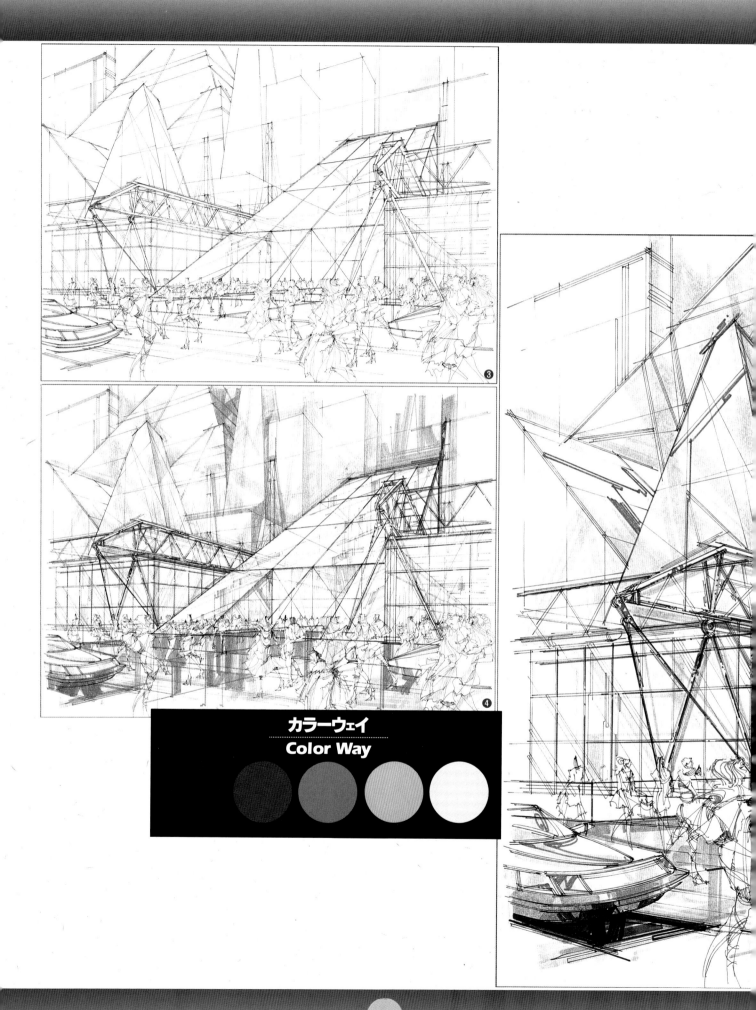

カラーウェイ
Color Way

❶
前出のケントボードの着彩のモノトーンパースの完成を
第2原図(トレーシングペーパーにモノクロコピーしたもの)に取る。
❷
第2原図の裏から薄いブルー、エメラルドグリーンで
ファサードのガラスの質感を意識しながらタッチを入れる。
直線的なタッチで表現する。
❸
さらに、タッチと濃淡にパンチをあてえる。
濃淡をはっきり描く。
❹
各色のチントマーカーで色の濃淡を表現しながら,
カラーブレンドで画面の上でマーカーをまぜ,
ニュアンスをあてえながら描き込む。
バックなどは、カラーブレンドを使い繊細に描き込む。
色鉛筆でもニュアンスをあてえながら描き込む。
ガラス、ステンレス、建築物などは直線のタッチで,
人物の点景は自由曲線でスピーディになおかつ、繊細に描く。
人物の色づかいなども,彩度や色相の強弱など
色のいろいろなニュアンスをあたえながら,
タッチの表情を豊かに描く。
❺
第2原図の裏と表両方よりタッチを入れる。
プロセス❹より少し濃いタッチで画面のニュアンスを強調し,

最後にポスターカラーのホワイトでハイライトを入れて
強調し,画面に光をあてえる。特にステンレス,
ガラスの質感は明暗のコントラストを強調すると,
感じがでる。これで完成である。

❶
Copy the previously completed monotone perspective Kentboard drawing onto the second original drawing (monochrome copied tracing paper).
❷
Apply some glass quality touches to the facade of the picture with light blue and emerald green. Express this with lineal touches.
❸
Add some punch to the picture with shading. Draw in the shading clearly.
❹
Use various tint markers to express the light and shade, and add some subtle nuances by mixing markers directly onto the drawing. Draw in the background in detail by blending colors. Use colored pencils as well to add special nuances. Draw in the glass, stainless steel and buildings with a lineal touch, and the people in freehand curvy lines speedily but nicely. Draw in the rich expressions of the people by arranging the brightness and hues in order to give off various nuances.
❺
Apply marker touches to the second original drawing from both sides. Add stronger touches than process #4 to emphasize the nuance of the drawing, and then add some light by inserting highlights with white poster color for accents. The texture of the stainless steel and glass can especially be expressed well by emphasizing the light and dark contrasts. The drawing is now complete.

ガラス,ステンレスなどのハイテックで硬質な素材の表現方法。
直線的タッチとブルー系,寒色系中心による表現方法。

Project 4

第2原図にマーカー着彩パース その1
透明ガラスでおおわれたハイテック風デザイン
Applying markers to the second original drawing. Perspective #1

A high-tech design covered with transparent glass.

The expression of hard materials with a degree of high technology such as glass and stainless steel. A lineal touch and cold colors are used to express the hard materials.

使 用 マ ー カ ー
Markers used in the drawing.

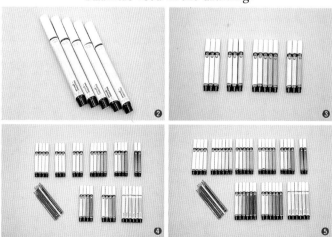

❶
No markers were used.
❷
209-M
304-M
317-M
351-M
365-M
❸
Tint 375 10%-40%
Tint 347 10%-40%
Tint process cyan 10%-80%
Tint violet 10%-40%
❹
Tint process yellow 20%-60%
Tint 375 10%-40%
Tint 347 10%-40%
Tint process cyan 10%-80%
Tint violet 10%-60%
Color Brenol
Tint process magenta 10%-60%
Tint warm red 10%-60%
100-M
489-M
182-M
250-M
162-M
176-M
6 color pencils.
❺
Tint 375 60%-100%
Tint 347 60%-80%
Tint process magenta 80%-100%
Tint warm red 80%-100%

プロセス
Process

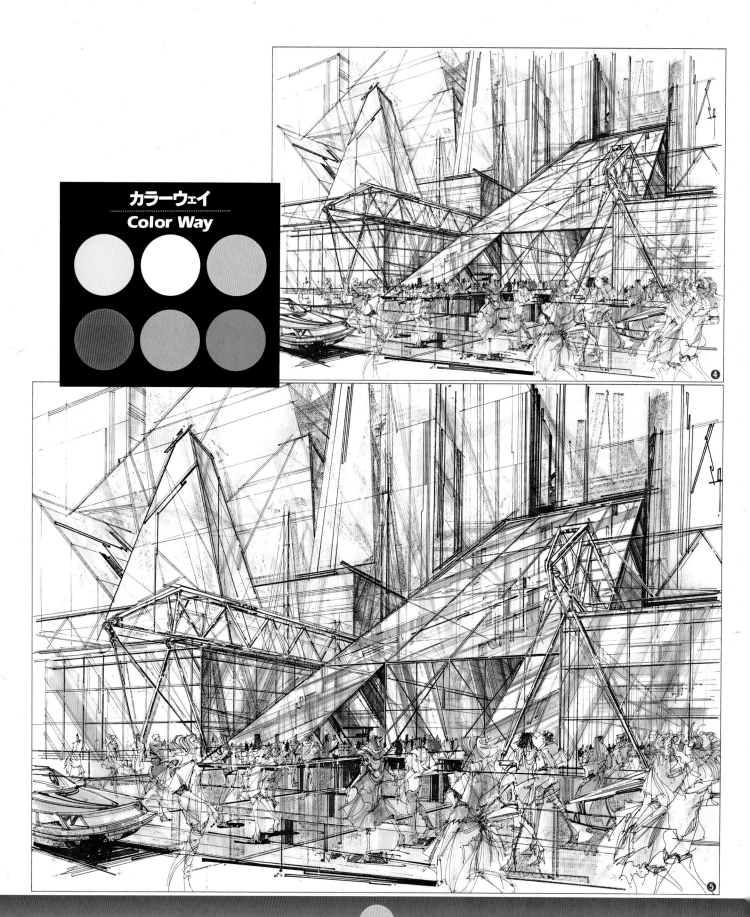

カラーウェイ
Color Way

❶
第2原図を取る。

❷
第2原図の裏から, 今回は最終的に建築物の質感に合わせ, 画面全体も派手にしたいので, ブルー系, 赤系の淡い色を画面全体に, 適当なバランスを見て描く。

❸
画面を派手にする。まず, 中央の建築ファサードのガラスの質感を意識しながらハイライトを残し, 明暗のコントラストを強調するように影の部分に濃いマーカーの色を入れていく。あくまでも直線的に入れていく。ガラスの中へのまわりの環境の映り込みも多少意識しながら, あらゆる方向からの直線的なタッチのリズムをあたえていく。チントマーカーによる色の幅, カラーブレンドによる部分的な色のまぜ合わせなど, 瞬時の画面のニュアンスを見ながら感覚的に入れていく。もう一つ, マーカーのタッチを入れていくとき, 下書きの線と違ったタッチのリズム, 流れを作って画面を構築していくことが重要である。いろいろ違ったリズム, ニュアンスをあたえ, 画面を作っていくことで, プロセスが進むにつれ, 画面に強さと新鮮さをあたえつづけることができる。プロセスが進むにつれてなおいっそう画面に輝き,

すなわち新鮮さをあたえるように描くことを心がける。それには, マンネリ化したタッチは入れないことである。人間の瞬間の感覚のひらめきを, 画面にあたえつづけるのである。したがって, 大まかなプロセスを意識しながら, ひらめきによる瞬間の画面への描き込みが, 新鮮なスケッチを生む重要な要素となる。それには瞬時に変化する画面を見ながら, 最初の計画にこだわらず, 描きながら画面の進め方を考えることが重要である。描き込みと, 画面の新鮮さを作ること, これを平行して意識し作業を進める。

❹
プロセス❸よりさらに濃いタッチを入れながら, 画面の強さをあたえ描き込む。中央の建築に重厚感と質感をあたえるために, トレーシングペーパーの両面から描き込む。その際, 表から描くときにはあまり強くこすると, コピーの線が溶けて画面がきたなくなってしまうので, サッと, あっさりと描く。全体的に描き込んだら, ポスターカラーのホワイトでガラス, 点景のハイライトにタッチを入れ完成である。

❶
Take a copy of the original drawing.
❷
Apply marker touches from the back of the copy of the original drawing. As the entire drawing will required a bright finish in order to match with the building, consider a reasonable balance and then add lighter shades of blue and red throughout.
❸
Draw in the picture with loud colors. Leave the highlights and draw in the shadows to emphasize the dark and light contrast with an awareness of the glass quality effect of the facade. Stay strictly to lineal touches when drawing. Apply various directional rhythms of lineal touches with a certain amount of consciousness of the reflections of the surrounding glass. Use your own sense when adding the color range of tint markers and the practical color blends while studying the momentary nuances of the overall impression. One more important method of marker technique is that one should add different touches of rhythm and flow from the lines of the rough sketch to insert a modicum of contrast into the picture. One can continue to assert one's individuality and a sense of freshness to the picture as

作品その1のバリエーションで, 色が鮮やかで派手にした表現方法。
色彩の画面上でのバランスの取り方が決め手。

Project 5

第2原図にマーカー着彩パース その2

外装が七色に光るガラスのカーテンウォールでおおわれたデザイン

Marker perspective #2 colored on the 2nd original drawing

An external design covered with a glass curtain wall reflecting 7 colors.

This is a variation of No. 4 with brighter colors.
The color balance within the picture.

使 用 マ ー カ ー
Markers used in the drawing.

❷

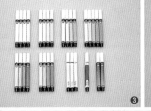
❸

❹

❶
No markers were used.
❷
290-M
317-M
250-M
489-M
❸
Tint process yellow 10%-60%
Tint 375 10%-60%
Tint 347 10%-60%
Tint process cyan 10%-80%
Tint violet 10%-60%
Tint warm red 10%-60%
351-M
304-M
365-M
300-M
Color blend
❹
Color pencils.

Rhodamine red F
485-F
Orange 021-F
144-F
116-F
Yellow F
396-F
375-F
347-F
300-F
Blue 072-F
Reflex blue F
259-F
Purple F
Process magenta 60%-100%
Warm red 80%-100%
Tint 375 80%
375 100%
Tint 347 80%
347 100%

the process advances. One should also strive to add a feeling of splendour and a precise freshness to the picture by avoiding the use of stereotyped strokes. Try to rely on your own sense of imaging. By doing this, one can produce new sketches through the medium of inspirational flashes. In order to achieve this it is important not only to draw along with the original plan, but also to consider the construction of the drawing and steadily alter it as you go along. It should be one's paramount objective to produce something original.

❹

Using darker marker strokes than in process #3, strengthen the picture. Stroke in from both sides of the tracing paper in order to give a heavy feeling and quality to the center building. When coloring in from the front, draw lightly as the copy ink will smudge and spoil the picture if pressed on too strongly. When the entire building has been finished, add the highlights on the glass and human figures with white poster color to complete.

カラーウェイ
Color Way

プロセス
Process

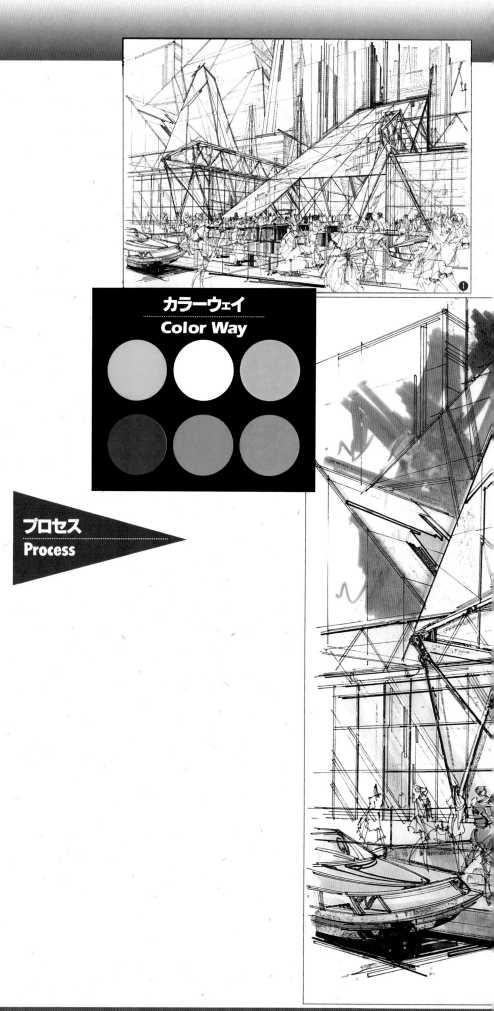

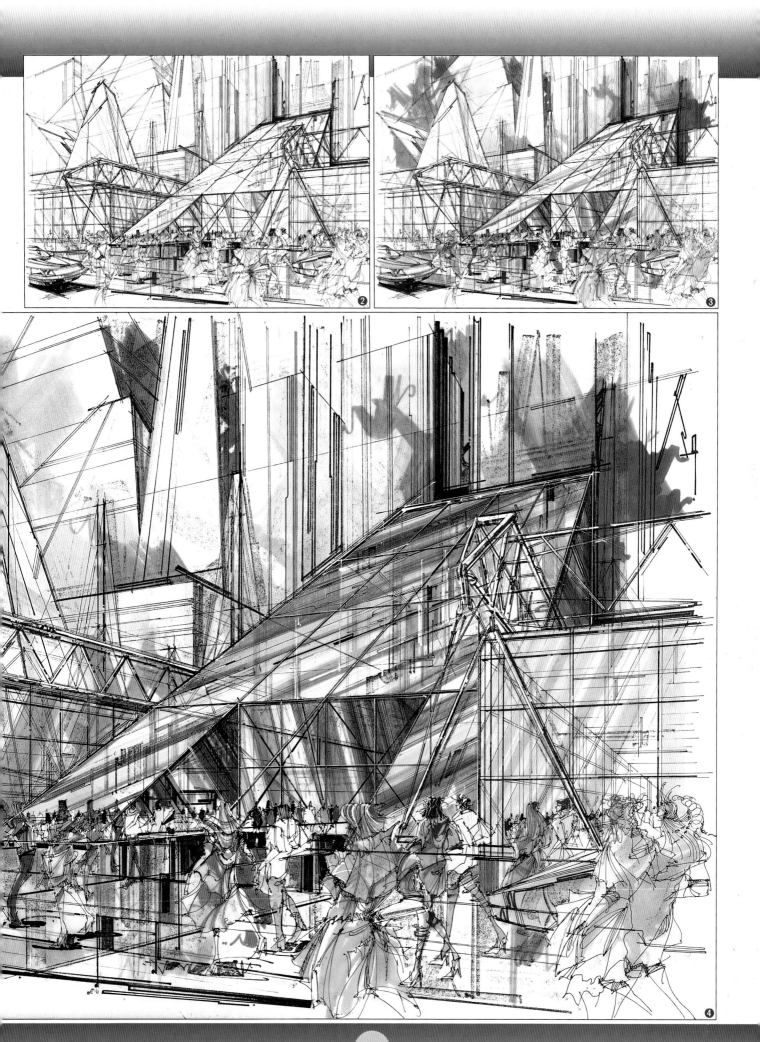

多目的型イベント＆コンサートホール：a：MULTIFARIOUS EVENT & CONCERT HALL
エアー・スタジオ：b：Air Studio
ガラスで構成された空間をもつ建築イメージのデッサン。：d：An architecture of glass sapce image drawing.
クールな感覚をバックのブルーにより強調する。 Accentuate the cool image of the glass
荒い調子でバックを描く。 by using blue in the background.
ガラスのこまかなニュアンスは色鉛筆で描く。 The background should be drawn in rough strokes.
Use colored pencils to draw in the fine nuances of the glass.

トータル・レジャーセンター :a: TOTAL LEISURE CENTER
エアー・スタジオ :b: Air Studio
このスケッチの空間イメージは, :d: The space image of this sketch flashed through
ある瞬間さっと目の前を通りすぎた　　　　my head and was gone very quickly, like a mirage.
蜃気楼のようなイメージを具体化した。　　Such images must be transfered to the illustratio
色彩とタッチにより即興的空間のイメージを　within a short a time period as possible.
瞬時にして表現できるのもマーカーの魅力といえる。　It is also necessary to express this feeling
of impromptu by adding colors
and touches as quickly as possible.

パブリック・スクエア&イベント・スペース : a : PUBLIC SQUARE & EVENT SPACE
エアー・スタジオ : b : Air Studio
この作品は図面のないイメージによる表現である。: d : This space has been drawn by an image expression
大空間のざわめきを without the benefit of an original plan.
ブルーを中心としたシンプルな色の流れにより表現する。 Simple flows of color based on blue
面相筆によりホワイトのハイライトを強めに入れて，ポイントを作る。 should be used to express the bustle
and confusion going on in the huge space.
Add some strong white highlights
with the use of fine brush in order to make a point.

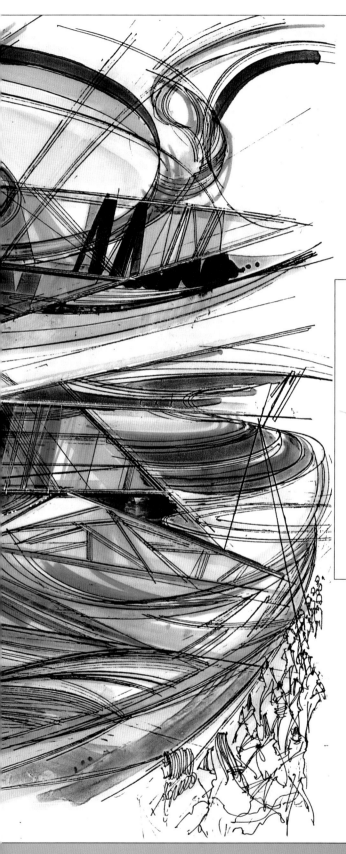

パフォーミング・スペース ファサード：a：PAFORMING SPACE-FACADE

レストラン ラン・ラン・ラン : a : RESTAURANT-RUN RUN RUN
エアー・スタジオ : b : Air Studio

アメリカン・レストラン 50'S : a : AMERICAN RESTAURANT 50'S
エアー・スタジオ : b : Air Studio

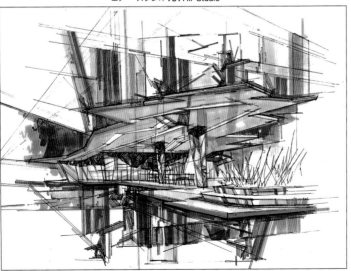

ディスコ ダンスステージ：a：DISCOTHEQUE DANCE STAGE
エアー・スタジオ：b：Air Studio
ガラスで作られたダンスステージ。：d：The glass stage of discotheque.
ガラスは淡いピンク系の色などが映り込み、 With the reflection made by such colors
カラフルなトーンを作り出す。 as pink shading, the glass should offer colorful tones.
その映り込みを美しく表現したい場合は、 Therefore, the main theme of this sketch is
直線的なタッチが有効。 to express the extensive image of the reflection
beautifully with the use of lineal touches.

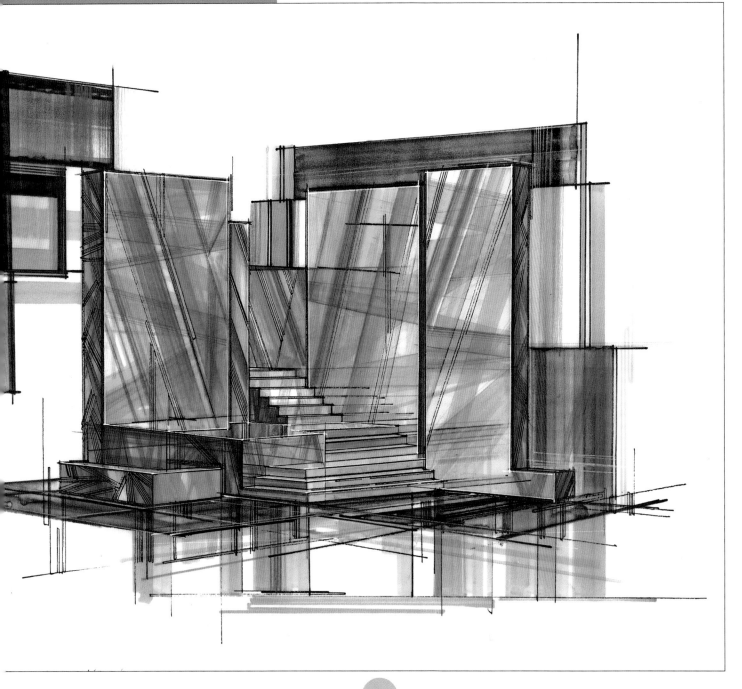

レストラン ピエロ・デラ・フランチェスカ：a
アース・ファクトリー：b

a : RESTAURANT-PIERO DELLA FRANCESCA
b : Earth Factory

カフェ・カーニバル：a：CAFE CARNIVAL

レストラン メロディー：**a**：RESTAURANT MELODY
エアー・スタジオ：**b**：Air Studio
このスケッチはバックの荒いタッチにより，：**d**：Add some nuance and rhythm to the touch
表現にはなやかなニュアンスとリズムをつける。in this sketch, too, by giving a rough feel to the background.
こまかなデザインよりも，大胆に画面全体のリズムで Bold rhythms should be made apparent
イメージを作り上げる。in the touches of the sketch instead of detailed design
in order to produce the required image.

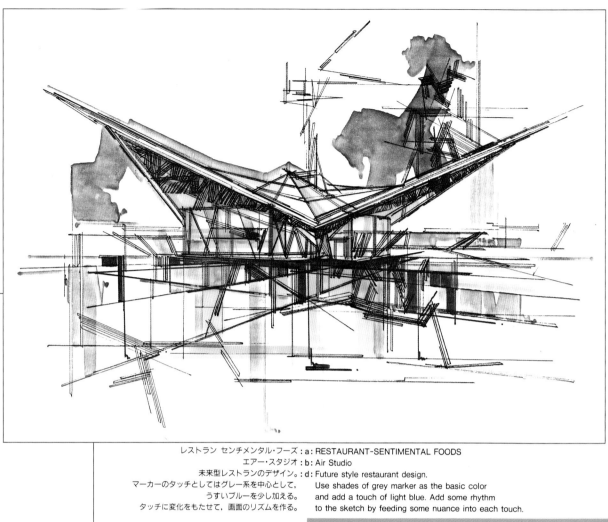

レストラン センチメンタル・フーズ：**a**：RESTAURANT-SENTIMENTAL FOODS
エアー・スタジオ：**b**：Air Studio
未来型レストランのデザイン。：**d**：Future style restaurant design.
マーカーのタッチとしてはグレー系を中心として、　Use shades of grey marker as the basic color
うすいブルーを少し加える。　and add a touch of light blue. Add some rhythm
タッチに変化をもたせて，画面のリズムを作る。　to the sketch by feeding some nuance into each touch.

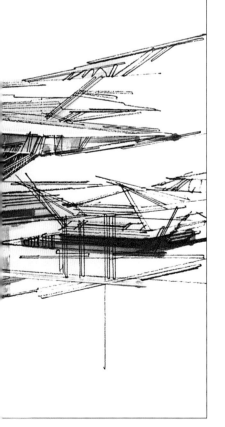

JR横浜駅ディスコ計画：a：JR YOKOHAMA STATION DISCOTHEUQE PLANNING
株式会社リンク，三原実：b：Link Co.,Ltd., Minoru Mihara
ディスコ・ビルのイメージ・スケッチ。：d：An image sketch of a discotheque building.
ドイツ表現主義風のデザイン。　　　　German style principles were used to design this sketch.
バックはビルのダイナミズムを表現するため、　Black marker was used for the background
黒のマーカーでしめる。　　　　in order to emphasize the dynamic feel of the building.
色彩はガラスのグリーンのみ。　　　　The only other color used here is green for the glass.
シンプルな構成にすることがポイント。　　Keep it as simple as possible.

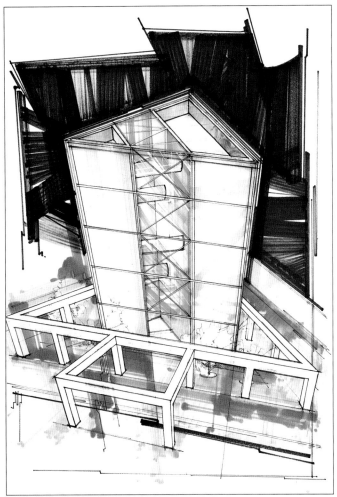

JR 横浜駅ディスコ計画 No.1：a：JR YOKOHAMA STATION DISCOTHEUQE PLANNING NO.1
株式会社リンク，三原実：b：Link Co.,Ltd., Minoru Mihara

ディスコ ファサード・イメージ：a：DISCOTHEQUE-FACADE IMAGE
エアー・スタジオ：b：Air Studio
このスケッチは具体的な形をリアルに表現するのではなく，：d：This sketch expresses an image of the building
イメージとしての建築を線と瞬間，by using lines and illusive strokes as
あたかも消えそうな幻のようなイメージを表現している。if they will soon fade and has pushed the concrete shape
淡いマーカーの色と色鉛筆の繊細なタッチで表現する。of the building into the background.
Use delicate touches of light color markers and colored pencils.

ギャラリー・ビル ファサード：a：GALLERY BUILDING-FACADE

ファサード・イメージ：a：FACADE IMAGE
アース・ファクトリー：b：Earth Factory

ファサード・イメージ：a：FACADE IMAGE
アース・ファクトリー：b：Earth Factory

ディスコ ファサード：a：DISCOTHEQUE-FACADE
エアー・スタジオ：b：Air Studio
砂漠の中にある廃虚風な：d：A mysterious space composition of a facade
ファサードのミステリアスな空間構成。廃虚のデザイン。　that looks like ruins standing in a desert.
色彩は茶系のみ。うすい茶系で表現する。　A modern design has been ventured
to treat the ruins with soft lines.
The only colors used are shades of brown.
Use light brown to express the ruins.

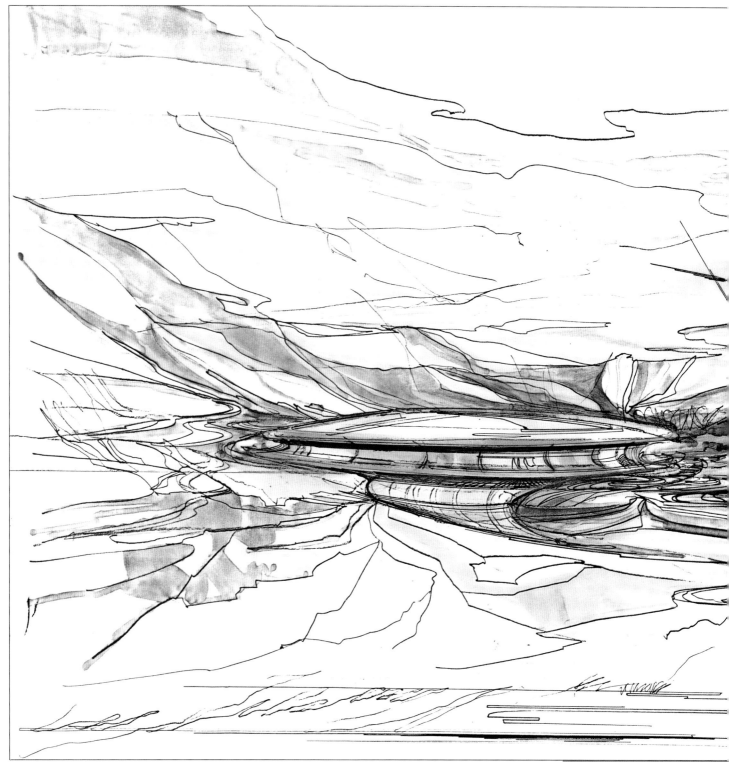

レストラン ライト : a : RESTAURANT-LIGHT
アース・ファクトリー : b : Earth Factory
空気の流れの中にうずもれながら、: d : An image of a building that is hidden beneath the flow of air,
浮かび上がるような建物をイメージした。 but at the same time manages to stand out.
色彩はパステルトーンをやわらかなタッチで、空気のように Pastel tones should be used to exoress the flow of the air.
よどまず流れるように画面を描く。白のヌキがポイントである。 The white waterfall is the main point of this sketch.

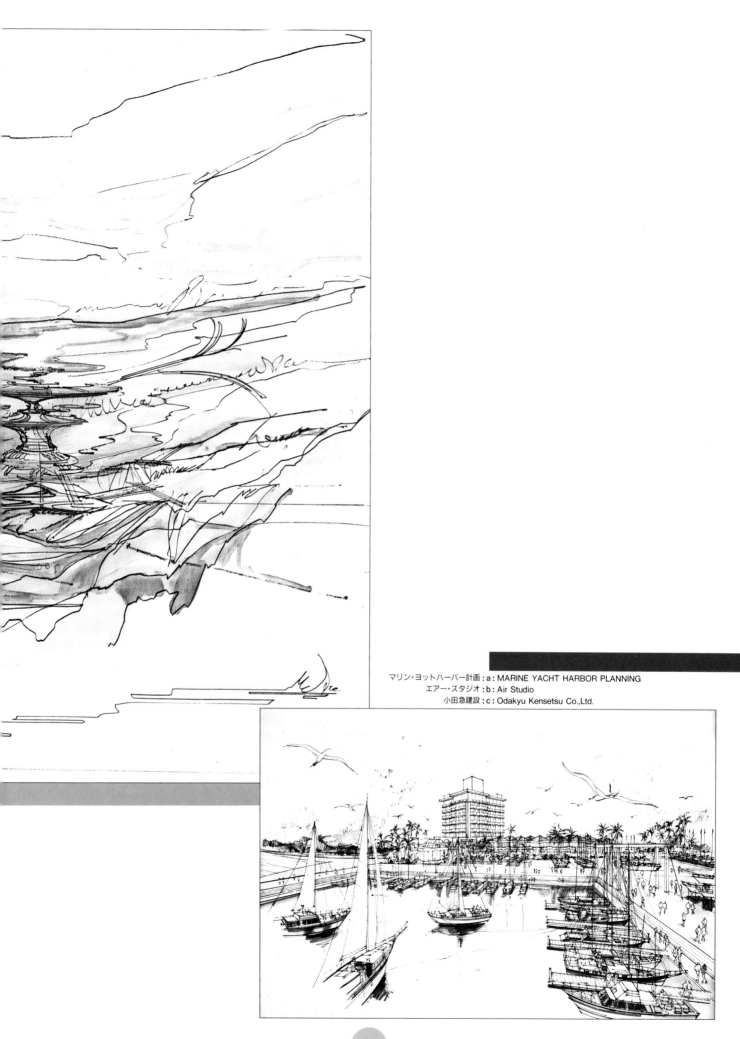

マリン・ヨットハーバー計画：a：MARINE YACHT HARBOR PLANNING
エアー・スタジオ：b：Air Studio
小田急建設：c：Odakyu Kensetsu Co.,Ltd.

センサー・コンプレックス パブリック・スペース：**a**：CENSOR COMPLEX-PUBLIC SPACE
エアー・スタジオ：**b**：Air Studio
小田急建設：**c**：Odakyu Kensetsu Co.,Ltd.

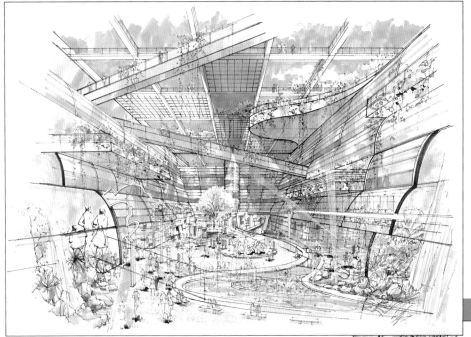

バンダイ・トレインランド レストラン：a：BANDAY TRAIN LAND-RESTAURANT
テツ・クリエイティブ：b：Tetsu Creative Co.,Ltd.
テツ・クリエイティブ：c：Tetsu Creative Co.,Ltd.

日本料理レストラン 桂：a：JAPANESE RESTAURANT KATSURA
エアー・スタジオ：b：Air Studio

池畔にたたずむ和風レセプションハウス

センサー・コンプレックス計画：a：CENSOR COMPLEX PLANNING
エアー・スタジオ：b：Air Studio
小田急建設：c：Odakyu Kensetsu Co.,Ltd.

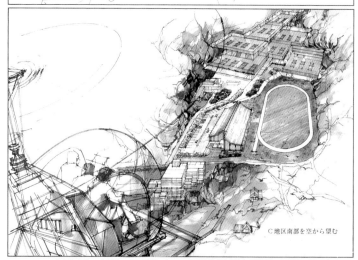

C地区南部を空から望む

レストラン，ホテル，テニスコート：a：RESTAURANT, HOTEL & TENNIS COURT

バンダイ・トレインランド レストラン：**a**：BANDAY TRAIN LAND-RESTAURANT
テツ・クリエイティブ：**b**：Tetsu Creative Co.,Ltd.
テツ・クリエイティブ：**c**：Tetsu Creative Co.,Ltd.

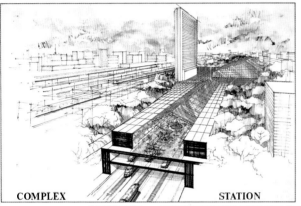

新宿駅南口計画：**a**：SHINJUKU STATION SOUTHERN PLANNING
エアー・スタジオ：**b**：Air Studio
小田急建設：**c**：Odakyu Kensetsu Co.,Ltd.

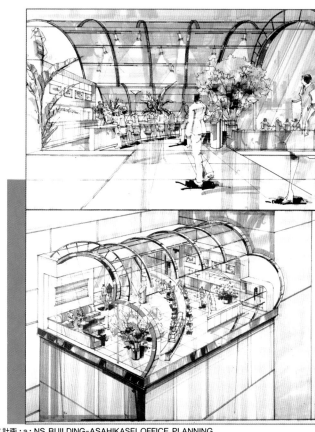

NS ビル 旭化成オフィス計画：a：NS BUILDING-ASAHIKASEI OFFICE PLANNING
エアー・スタジオ：b：Air Studio

バンダイ・トレインランド：a：BANDAY TRAIN LAND
テツ・クリエイティブ：b：Tetsu Creative Co.,Ltd.
テツ・クリエイティブ：c：Tetsu Creative Co.,Ltd.

スポーツ・ショップ カンフー : a : SPORTS SHOP-GONG FU
コンセプト・キュー : b : Concept Q Co.,Ltd.
コンセプト・キュー : c : Concept Q Co.,Ltd.

ディスコ レイラ : a : DISCOTHEQUE-LAYLA
コンセプト・キュー，エアー・スタジオ : b : Concept Q Co.,Ltd., Air Studio
コンセプト・キュー : c : Concept Q Co.,Ltd.

バンダイ・トレインランド : a : BANDAY TRAIN LAND
テツ・クリエイティブ : b : Tetsu Creative Co.,Ltd.
テツ・クリエイティブ : c : Tetsu Creative Co.,Ltd.

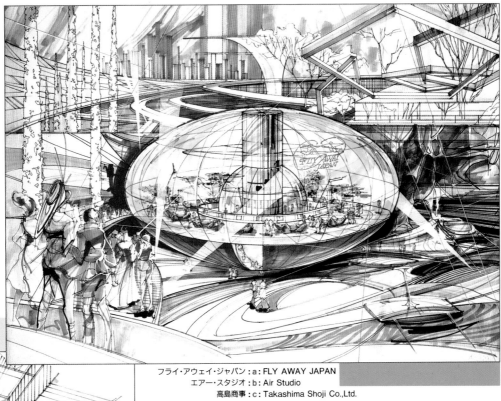

フライ・アウェイ・ジャパン：a：FLY AWAY JAPAN
エアー・スタジオ：b：Air Studio
高島商事：c：Takashima Shoji Co.,Ltd.

フライ・アウェイ・ジャパン：a：FLY AWAY JAPAN
エアー・スタジオ：b：Air Studio
高島商事：c：Takashima Shoji Co.,Ltd.

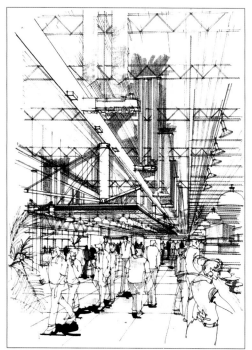

バンダイ・トレインランド インテリア : a : INTERIOR OF BANDAY TRAIN LAND
テツ・クリエイティブ : b : Tetsu Creative Co.,Ltd.
テツ・クリエイティブ : c : Tetsu Creative Co.,Ltd.

レストレラン&カフェバー ステージ Y2 : a : RESTAURANT & CAFE BAR-STAGE Y2
和田裕設計室 : b : Yutaka Wada Space Planning Office
ヨックモック : c : Yoku-Moku Co.,Ltd.

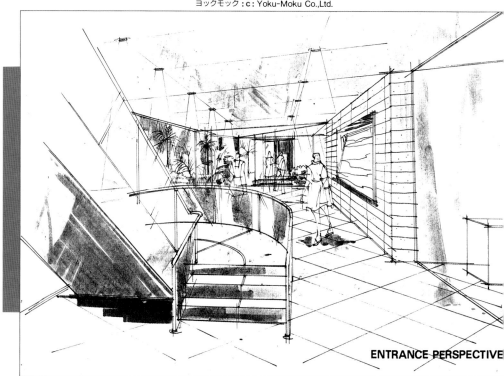

ENTRANCE PERSPECTIVE

シアター＆オフィス・インテリア：a：THEATER & OFFICE INTERIOR
プロポーション：b：Proportion

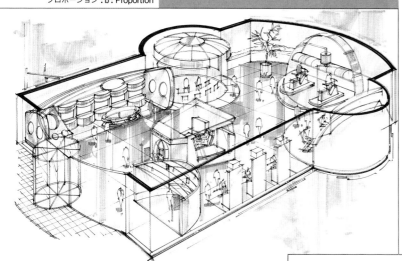

シアター＆オフィス・インテリア：a：THEATER & OFFICE INTERIOR
プロポーション：b：Proportion
プロポーション：c：Proportion

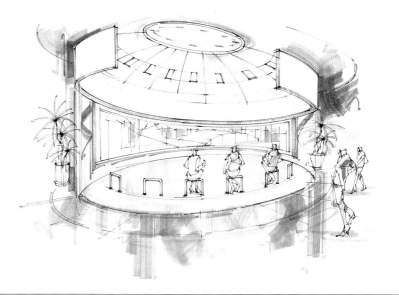

レストレラン＆カフェバー ステージ Y2：a：RESTAURANT & CAFE BAR-STAGE Y2
和田裕設計室：b：Yutaka Wada Space Planning Office
ヨックモック：c：Yoku — Moku Co.,Ltd.

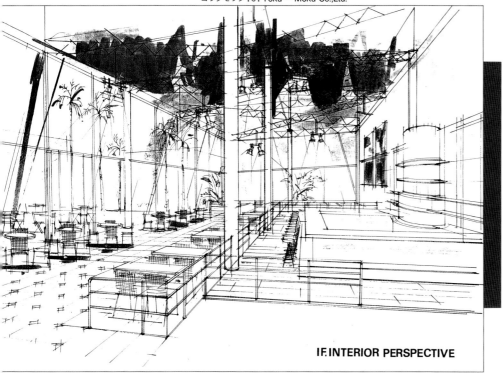

I.F. INTERIOR PERSPECTIVE

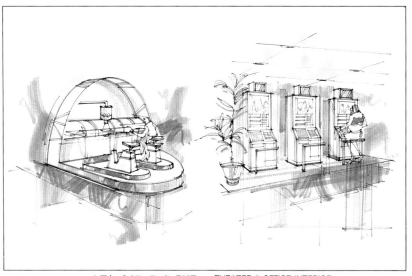

シアター&オフィス・インテリア：a：THEATER & OFFICE INTERIOR
プロポーション：b：Proportion
プロポーション：c：Proportion

シアター&オフィス・インテリア：a：THEATER & OFFICE INTERIOR
プロポーション：b：Proportion
プロポーション：c：Proportion

シアター&オフィス・インテリア：a：THEATER & OFFICE INTERIOR
プロポーション：b：Proportion
プロポーション：c：Proportion

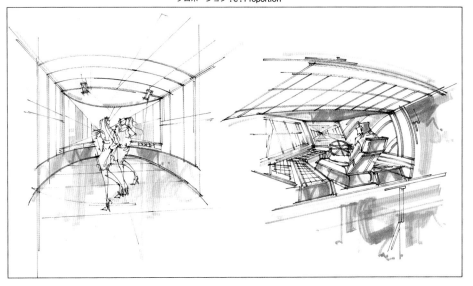

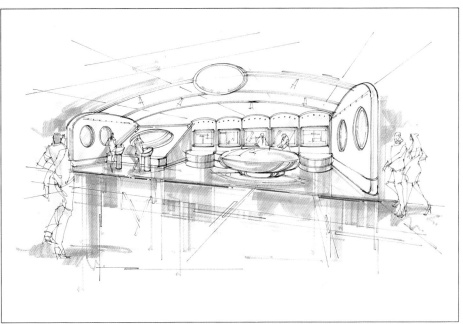

シアター&オフィス・インテリア：a：THEATER & OFFICE INTERIOR
プロポーション：b：Proportion
プロポーション：c：Proportion

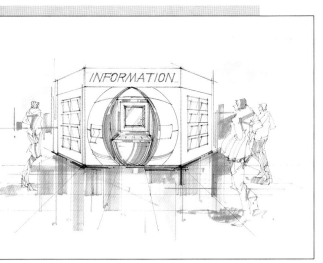

シアター&オフィス・インテリア：a：THEATER & OFFICE INTERIOR
プロポーション：b：Proportion
プロポーション：c：Proportion

シアター&オフィス・インテリア：a：THEATER & OFFICE INTERIOR
プロポーション：b：Proportion
プロポーション：c：Proportion

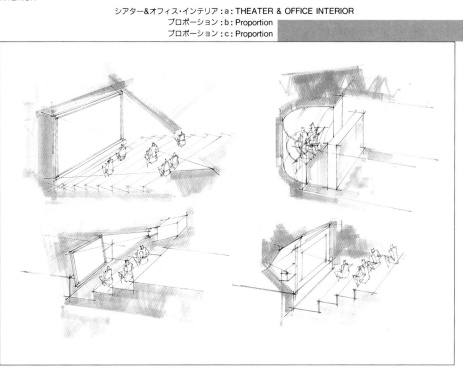

サーキット・クラブハウス : **a** : CIRCUIT CLUBHOUSE
オムニバス : **b** : Omnibus

ゴルフ・クラブハウス&レストラン : **a** : GOLF CLUBHOUSE & RESTAURANT
エアー・スタジオ : **b** : Air Studio
小田急建設 : **c** : Odakyu Kensetsu Co.,Ltd.

第三章
現代的な
リアル・イメージスケッチ
How to Employ
A Realistic Touch to Subjects.
Chapter 3

① 広角的にアングルをとり，墨入れする。
ミラーの中の映り込みや，床のパターンもしっかり描き込む。
特にシャンデリアはこまかすぎるぐらいに，
ガッチリデッサンし描き込む。
2階の手すりのパーテーションのレリーフなども，
細いサインペンで繊細に描き込む。
②
クールグレー，ウォームグレーのすべてを使用して
グレーの明暗で下地を作る。
要領は，後出のファサードのプロセスで述べるが，
ミラーの映り込みはしっかり描き込む。
そして天井もグレーの濃い色でしめる。
全体に，ウォーム系とクール系の両方で描き込む。
右側の壁画は，コンクリートの打ちっぱなしなので，
この段階でその質感を表現してしまう。階段は
この2階と1階の高さ，ホールの前後の距離感を表現する
重要なポイントなので強めに，しっかり立体感を表現する。
③
ブルー系とグリーン系の淡いトーンでガラスとミラーを，
直線的に描き込む。グレーの下地の上に
重ねるように描き込む。
④
柱や床の木調の質感を描き込む。

グレーの下地の上から描き，少し渋めで
落ち着きのあるちょうどいい感じに色を決める。
カラーブレンドで，部分的に画面上で色をまぜ合わせながら
描いてもおもしろい。
あまりこすりすぎると，色がにごるので気をつけるように。
⑤
エンジのベッチンの垂れ幕とカーペットをエンジ，紫，茶，
濃紺などを塗り，重ねトーンをしては抑えぎみに表現する。
床のパターンも，しっかり描き込む。
シャンデリアには，淡いイエローを入れる。奥のスペースに
あるイス，テーブル，その他に少し色気を入れる。
最後に，ポスターカラーのホワイトで，
シャンデリアの光の方向をリアルに表現する。
この光の表現は，たとえば実際に写真に写してみると
光の表現がわかるが，
光源から十字に光が伸びるように描くと良い。
それから床のパターン，ガラスやミラーのハイライト，
その他のハイライトにも，ホワイトを入れる。
レリーフのハイライトは白で明るいところを彫刻の形を
しっかり作るように，色を盛り上げる感じで描くと
感じが出る。これで完成である。

① Take a wide angle and apply the inking.

Draw in the reflection in the mirror and the pattern of the floor precisely. The sketch of the chandelier should be drawn in almost too much detail. The relief of the hand-rail partition on the 2nd floor should also be drawn in great detail with felt-tip pen.
②
Use all of the shades connected to cool grey and warm grey to produce the ground coat with grey light and shade. Brush in the reflection in the mirror firmly in the same style mentioned in the picture of the facade. Brace up the picture by using dark grey on the ceiling. Color in the entire space with warm and cool grey. The quality of the wall painting on the right should be expressed at this stage as having a concrete finish. A considerably strong cubic expression should be given to the stairs as it is important to impart the height of the 2nd and 1st floors and the distance of the hall from one end to the other.
③
Using light tones of blue and green, color in the glass and mirror directly as if brushing on

使 用 マ ー カ ー
Markers used in the drawing.

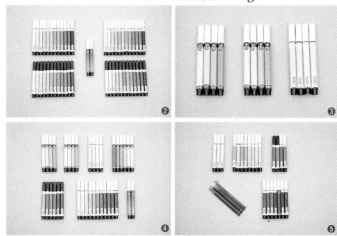

①	
No markers were used.	139-M
②	173-M
Cool grey 1M-11M	484-M
Extra black M	464-M
Warm grey 1M-11M	469-M
Extra black M	497-M
Cool grey 1F-11F	Color blend.
Extra black F	⑤
Warm grey 1F-11F	475-M
Extra black F	459-M
Color blend.	100-M
③	319-M
Process cyan 10%-60%	243-M
Tint-347 10%-60%	170-M
290-M	251-M
304-M	148-M
317-M	176-M
351-M	162-M
④	182-M
471 10%-100%	327-F
465-F	Green F
471-F	327-M
132-F	340-M
154-F	485-M
168-F	Purple M
477-F	265-M
155-M	259-M
134-M	Violet 100%
141-M	Reflex blue M
472-M	477-M
465-M	Color pencils.

top of the grey ground coat.

❹
Brush in the wooden quality of the pillars and the floor. The color will be perfectly sober if stroked on top of the ground coat, and will produce an enjoyable blend. Be careful not to rub too much as the colors will smudge.

❺
Paint in the deep red drop curtain and carpet in deep red, purple, brown and navy blue with rather quieter tones.Draw in the detail of the floor pattern as well. Apply bright yellow to the chandelier. Add a little color to the chairs, tables and other items at the back of the space. Lastly, express the direction of the chandelier's light with white poster color as realistically as possible. A brief look at a photograph will give one the best idea for expressing light flows, and here it is better to draw it away from the sauce of the light. Add highlights to the floor pattern, glass, mirror and other items. For the highlighting of the relief, it will be more effective to draw along the light areas of the statue in white to help it stand out. The picture is now complete.

プロセス
Process

カラーウェイ
Color Way

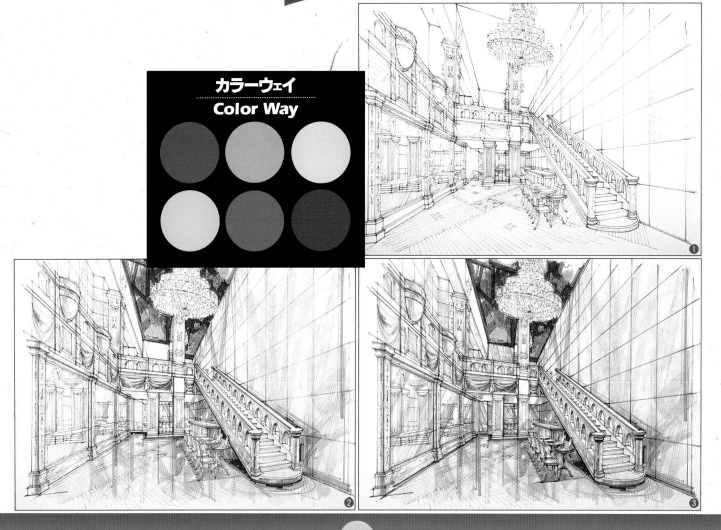

❶
墨入れ完了。
❷
下地のグレートーンで空間, 明暗, 質感, 立体感などの
すべて表現する。特にミラーは
中の映り込みと表面の反射面は最初に中を描き,
そのうえで表面の反射の明暗を描くと感じが出る。
❸
前出のダンスホールと同じような要項で
ミラー, ガラスを描き込み,
そのあとで木調の柱や壁面の質感やイスを描き込む。
❹
ベッチンのエンジの垂れ幕を描く。左側の通路と
右側レストランのカーペットの色が対称的なので,
この色の対比がスケッチの大きなポイントになる。
カーペットの文様は水彩色具や色鉛筆などを使用し,
こまかくしっかり描き込む。
イスやテーブルのハイライトなどを意識し,
全体にホワイトを入れ完成である。

❶
The inking is complete.
❷
Express the space, lightness and darkness,
the quality of the materials and its cubic
shape with grey tones in a ground coat.
The image in the mirror and the reflections
on the surface of the mirror will especially
look effective if the light and shade are
drawn in after the ground coat.
❸
Brush in the mirror and glass in the same
way as described for the process in the
dance hall. Then draw in the quality of the
wooden pillars, the wall material and the
chairs.
❹
Draw in the deep red velvet drop curtains.
The color of the carpet in the corridor to the
right contrasts with the carpet in the
restaurant on the left and therefore becomes
a prime point for this sketch. The pattern of
the carpet should be drawn in great detail
using water colors or colored pencils.
Add white to the entire picture and complete
the highlights on the tables and chairs with a
certain amount of consciousness.

基本的にダンスホールの2階なので, デザインも関連性があるが
カーペットなどに色のポイントが出る。

Project 7

原宿ディスコ グレースキャステル
レストランバー・スペース
Harajuku Discoteque Grace Castle
Restaurant Bar Space.
Basically this space is designed in the same style as the
dance hall as it is situated on the 2nd floor, but this time
the design point is placed on the color of the carpet.

使 用 マ ー カ ー
. . . .
Markers used in the drawing.

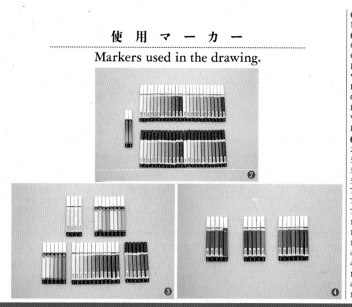

❶	484-M
No markers were used.	469-M
❷	497-M
Color blend	477-M
Cool grey 1M-11M	465-F
Extra black M	132-F
Warm grey 1M-11M	154-F
Extra black M	471-F
Cool grey 1M-11M	168-F
Extra black	477-F
Warm grey 1F-11F	❹
Extra black F	485-M
❸	Purple M
290-M	265-M
304-M	259-M
317-M	Violet 100%
351-M	Reflex blue M
Tint process cyan 10%-60%	548-M
Tint-347 10%-60%	300-M
Tint-471 10%-100%	Process blue M
155-M	279-M
134-M	158-M
141-M	Super warm red M
472-M	206-M
465-M	173-M
139-M	484-M
464-M	469-M
173-M	497-M

プロセス
Process

カラーウェイ
Color Way

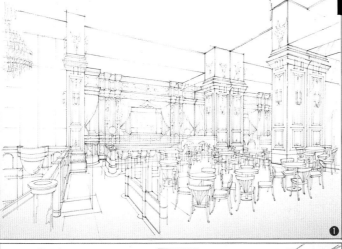

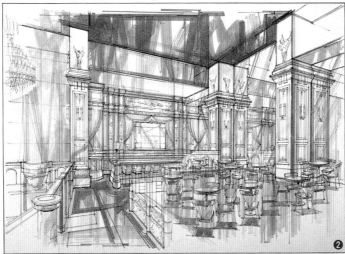

❶
墨入れ完了。

❷
グレーで下地を作る。カウンター天板の下と
イスの下は画面を絞めるため, 影を強調して描くといい。
天上と壁面の際やカーテンのアウトラインも強めに描く。

❸
木調の質感を描き込む。
要領は前出レストラン・バー スペースのプロセスと同じ。
イスの背面の文様やカウンターの側面は,
トーンに幅をもたせ, グラデーションでじっくり描き込む。
床の大理石に, ベージュをうすく描き込む。
明るいところと暗いところ二つの描き方は
はっきり分けたほうがいい。
明るいところは彩度がはっきりした表現, すなわち,
グレートーンの上に色がついたマーカーを重ねるときは
あっさりのせる。暗いところでは,
グレーの上に色をのせるとき, 画面上でカラーブレンドを
まぜ合せたりして, わざと色をにごらせ
彩度を落とすというテクニックを意識して使うといい。
このへんのこまかなニュアンスの作り方は, 経験からかなり
の即興的テクニックをその人なりに発見できると思う。

❹
カウンター前の色ガラス, 床のパターンを描き込む。

グラフィカルにしっかりきちっと描き込む。
カーテンのエンジ, カーペット, ガラスのブルー,
床のパターンを描き込み, ホワイトを入れる。天上などの
ホワイトの直線的タッチは, 多少荒めにスピーディに描く。
正面のレリーフなんかも, 白で形をおこすように描く。
これで完成である。

❶
The inking completed.

❷
Paint in the ground coat with grey. It will look more effective if the shadows under the counter-top and chairs are drawn in a darker shade to brace up the picture. The border between the ceiling and walls, and the outline of the curtains should also be drawn in darker shades.

❸
Do not draw in the wooden parts in the same way as mentioned in the previous processes. Take time to brush in the patterns on the backs of the chairs and sides of the counter using a wide range of color graduation. Add beige lightly to the marble stone on the floor. A completely different method of

drawing is recommendable for the light and dark sections of this picture. The light sections should be expressed in disctinct chromas.
In other words, simply add color markers to the grey tones of the ground coat. When applying color to the darker sections, such techniques as color opaqueness or decreasing chroma by color blending should be considered during the actual process of drawing.
One is likely to discover one's individual character through the technique of producing subtlely improvised techniques during this experience.

❹
Draw in the colored glass at the fore of the counter and the floor pattern. Draw this graphically and precisely. Paint the curtains in deep red, the carpet and glass in blue and the floor pattern in white. Apply some white lineal strokes to the ceiling and other elements with small, rough and speedy strokes. Use white to draw along the shape of the relief on the bookcase in the front in order to raise the shape. The picture is now complete.

このバーコーナーも, 基本的には連続的デザインである。
ポイントは, バーカウンターとイスのバランス。

原宿ディスコ グレースキャステル

Project 8 バー・コーナー

Harajuku Discoteque Grace Castle

Bar Corner.

Basically the design of this bar is connected with the other spaces, but the design point here is placed on the balance between the bar counter and the chairs.

使 用 マ ー カ ー
Markers used in the drawing.

❷

❸

❹

❶	168-F
No markers were used.	477-F
❷	❹
Color blend	290-M
Cool grey 1M-11M	304-M
Extra Black M	317-M
Warm grey 1M-11M	351-M
Extra black M	Tint-347 10%-60%
Cool grey 1F-11F	Tint process cyan 10%-60%
Extra black F	Tint 10%-60%
Warm grey 1F-11F	279-M
Extra black F	Process blue M
❸	300-M
Tint-471 10%-100%	279-F
155-M	Process cyan 2-M
134-M	Process blue F
141-M	206-M
472-M	Saper Warm Red M
465-M	485-M
139-M	173-M
464-M	484-M
469-M	158-M
477-M	Purple M
497-M	265-M
465-F	Violet 100%
132-F	259-M
154-F	Reflex blue M
471-F	

カラーウェイ
Color Way

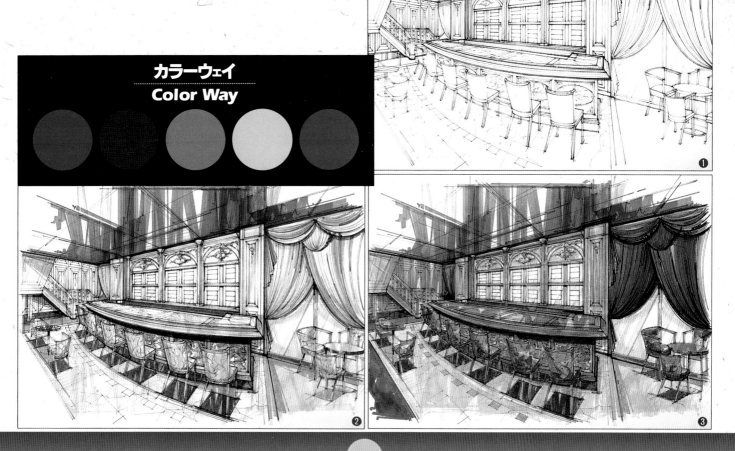

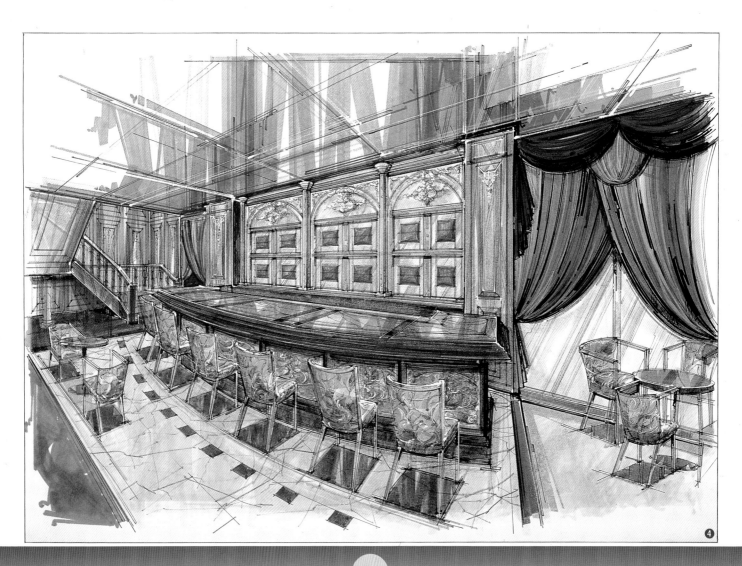

❶
真ん中の入口部を残し、グレーの壁と
そのまわりの黒い部分を荒いタッチで画面構成する。
ファサードが短調なので、まわりの黒いタッチは荒く、
そしていろいろな方向からさまざまなニュアンスのタッチで
画面をしめると画面に躍動感が出る。
❷
入口まわりに色を入れる。
要領は今までのプロセスと同じであるが、この画面では
入口まわり以外はすべて、モノトーンという短調な構成なので、
入口まわりの濃いグレーのタッチが
唯一画面にニュアンスをあたえる要素なので、
画面をしめるタッチが重要なポイントになる。
このようなタッチは、何枚もの練習でよりいいタッチを
さがしながら描いてもらいたい。完成である。

❶
Leaving the extrance section in the center,
produce this picture by applying rough
touches to the grey wall and its surrounding
black to brace up the picture. As the facade
is rather dull, it is possible to produce a lively
motion in the drawing by bracing up the
surroundings with black touches of subtle
nuance from various angles.
❷
Insert color into the surrounding door areas.
The essentials of the process are the same
as in the previous process, but as the picture
consists of a monotonous monotone, with the
exception of the entrance, this bracing up is
an important point to add the necessary
nuances to the overall impression.
Such work will need lots of practice to
produce the effect one wishes. The picture is
now complete.

このファサードのパースは、コンクリート打ちっぱなしの
木調のドアとまわりの大理石と2本のポールを、
イメージであっさりと表現したもので、
プロセスではモノトーンと彩色の2パターンだけを示す。

原宿ディスコ グレースキャステル

Project 9　ファサード

Harajuku Discoteque Grace Castle

Facade.

This facade has been simply drawn by expressing the
images of the untreated concrete, the wooden door and
its surrounding marble, and the two poles.
Only two patterns of monotone and chroma are indicated
in the process.

使 用 マ ー カ ー
Markers used in the drawing.

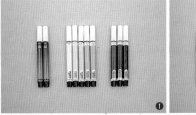

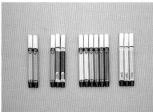

❶
Color blend
Cool grey 1M-5M
Cool grey 10M-11M
Extra M
❷
Tint 347 40%-60%
Tint process cyan 60%
Tint 279-M
Tint 548-M
Tint 471 10%-100%
155-M
134-M
141-M

カラーウェイ
Color Way

❶❷
ケントボードにモノトーンのグレーの濃淡を作り,
それでモノトーンによるボードパースを作る。
❸
第2原図を取る。
❹
全体にブルー系による水のイメージを作るため,
チントマーカーの幅を保たせながら,

おもにトレーシングペーパーの裏から塗り込む。
❺
ブルーの濃いアクセントをつける。
その際に,トレーシングペーパーの表から塗ると,
パンチがきいて鮮やかになる。
❻
淡い暖色系のトーンを全体に塗り込む。
❼

壁面アートのポイントに強い赤系を塗る。
こまかなアクセントを色鉛筆で表現し,描き込む。
ブルー系のインテリアの中にポイントとして,
赤系で少しアクセントをつけ表現する。完成である。

❶❷
First, create shades on the Kentboard in
monochrome grey and then draw in the board

このスケッチは,現在東京の駒沢の住宅地と駒沢公園の前に立地し,
1989年に放映されたテレビドラマ,「抱きしめたい」にも
たびたび登場した,話題のレストランである。
インテリアは,巨大な壁面アートを中心にした
ギャラリー風レストランバーである。
インテリア全体が海と水のイメージで,濃淡の幅をもつブルー系で
イメージされており,壁面アートは地中海や南海の海の夕日と,
それに反射する水面のイメージの変化する瞬間をとらえた
トータルな水のイメージ,海のイメージのインテリアである。
アート性とファッション性が現代の風俗とジョイントし,
単に,商業施設としてのレストランの枠を大きく越えたものである。
また,テレビドラマ「抱きしめたい」の舞台の中心となり,
最先端の現代の東京の若者のライフスタイルのイメージとしても,
浅野ゆう子,浅野温子のダブル浅野とともに,

このイング駒沢は,一つのライフスタイルのイメージの提案という,
1989年最高の社会現象にもなった。
現代の日本の中心の東京とインテリアブームと,
テレビとファッション性のジョイントの,イメージの1つの形である。
ファッション性とアート性と風俗のおしゃれなイメージこそが,
このスケッチのポイントになる。
おしゃれな男女のカップルがこのレストランの中に入り,
自分がドラマの浅野ゆう子になりきり,そのステージで
現代のおしゃれなドラマの主人公を演じる女優になる。
そのような,おしゃれ感覚を期待させるスケッチが,
その後のすべての方向性を決めるので,大変重要なポイントなのである。
イメージディレクターとの打合わせにより,スケッチの方向性を決め,
アートを中心に水のイメージのこのレストランを描く。

Project 10

フィッシャーマンズワーフ
ギャラリー＆レストランバー イング駒沢 内装

Fisherman's Wharf

Gallery and restaurant, bar ; Ing Komazawa Interior.

This is a sketch of the restaurant located in front of the
Komazawa residential area and Komazawa park in Tokyo
that has recently become a conversation topic owing to its
frequent appeerence in the sketches of a television
program called "I wanna hold you tight". Interior-wise,
it has been made into a gallery-type restaurant bar with a
huge wall mural as its central figure. Our studio was even
requested to supply the mural. As the entire interior has
been arranged in a wide range of blue shades depicting
images of sea and water, it was decided to paint an
image of the evening sun in the Mediterranean or South
Pacific with the surface of the water reflecting it.
This is an interior totally filled with water and sea
images.
Indeed, this restaurant has managed to combine art and
fashion with modern manners and customs and greatly
exceeded the definition of a restaurant as a commercial
facility.
The Ing Komazawa has created the biggest social

phenomenon in 1989 by proposing a life-style image of
Tokyo that attracts young people who are, in turn,
attracted to the buzzing life of Tokyo, as well as the two
Asano actresses - Yuko Asano and Atsuko Asano - who
are the central figures of a TV drama and who lead the
life of modern young Tokyoites. It is an image of a
modern age in which present-day Japan's central city,
Tokyo, and the boom in interior decoration and fashion
have been brought together. This true fashion, art and
smart image of manners and customs are the main points
for this sketch. A smartly-dressed couple enter the
restaurant. The girl is identified as the star of the drama
and becomes an actress who plays the role of a
modernly-dressed heroine. It is important to draw the
sketch including such expectation as it will decide the
entire direction in later stages. The direction of the sketch
should be fixed by arrangement with the image director,
and the water image of the restaurant should be drawn
with art as its central figure.

perspective in monotones.

❸
Take a copy of the original.

❹
In order to create the image of water in blue, chiefly paint in from the back of the tracing paper by using a wide range of tint markers.

❺
Add the accents in dark blue. The color will become stronger and more vivid by painting in the right side of the tracing paper.

❻
Use light and warm color tones to spread in the entire board.

❼
Paint in the point of the wall mural in a strong shade of red. Use colored pencils to express small accent details. This is a blue interior expressed with a little red as an accent point. The work is now complete.

使 用 マ ー カ ー

Markers used in the drawing.

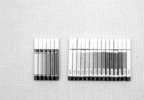

❹❺

❻❼

❹❺
Process cyan tint 10%-100%
279-M
Process cyan 2-M
Process cyan blue M
300-M
Blue 072-M

290-M
304-M
317-M
319-M

❻❼
185 tint 10%-100%
134-M
475-M
250-M
243-M
176-M
170-M
251-M
265-M
Purple M
Rhodamine red M
185-M
206-M
021-M
Process yellow 2-M

プロセス
Process

カラーウェイ
Color Way

❷

❶

❸

①②③
ボードに下書きし, 濃淡のグレーマーカーにより彩色。
④
第2原図を取る。
⑤⑥
ブルー系で空, プール, 建物を彩色する。
⑦
完成である。

①②③
Draw a rough sketch on the board and shade it in with grey markers.
④
Take a copy of the original.
⑤⑥
Color in the sky, the pool and the building in shades of blue.
⑦
The work is now complete.

プロセス
Process

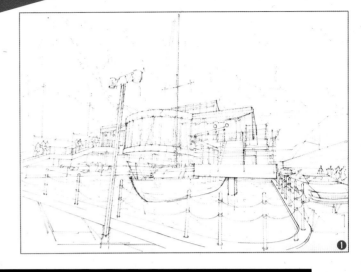

①

このレストランの外観の特徴として, ファサードの前面に巨大なブルーのプールを配置し, 水面に白いヨットを浮かべせている。パースのイメージとしては,

サンセットタイムの中に浮かび上がる建物を海のイメージで描きたい。東京の駒沢の住宅地のイメージを忘れて, あたかも, カリフォルニアの黄昏どきのヨットハーバーのイメージで描きたい。

フィッシャーマンズワーフ

ギャラリー＆レストランバー イング駒沢 外装

Project 11

Fisherman's Warf

Gallery and restaurant, bar ; Ing Komazawa Exterior.

As a special feature on the exterior of this restaurant a huge blue pool with a white yacht sailing across it was painted on the main facade. As a perspective image it should conjour up a feeling of a seaside building to stand out during the sunset. The image of the Komazawa residential area should be replaced with an image of a Californian yacht harbour in the evening sun.

使 用 マ ー カ ー
Markers used in the drawing.

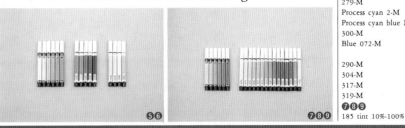

⑤⑥   ⑦⑧⑨

⑤⑥		134-M
Process cyan tint 10%-100%		475-M
279-M		250-M
Process cyan 2-M		243-M
Process cyan blue M		176-M
300-M		170-M
Blue 072-M		251-M
		265-M
290-M		Purple M
304-M		Rhodamine red M
317-M		185-M
319-M		206-M
⑦⑧⑨		021-M
185 tint 10%-100%		Process yellow 2-M

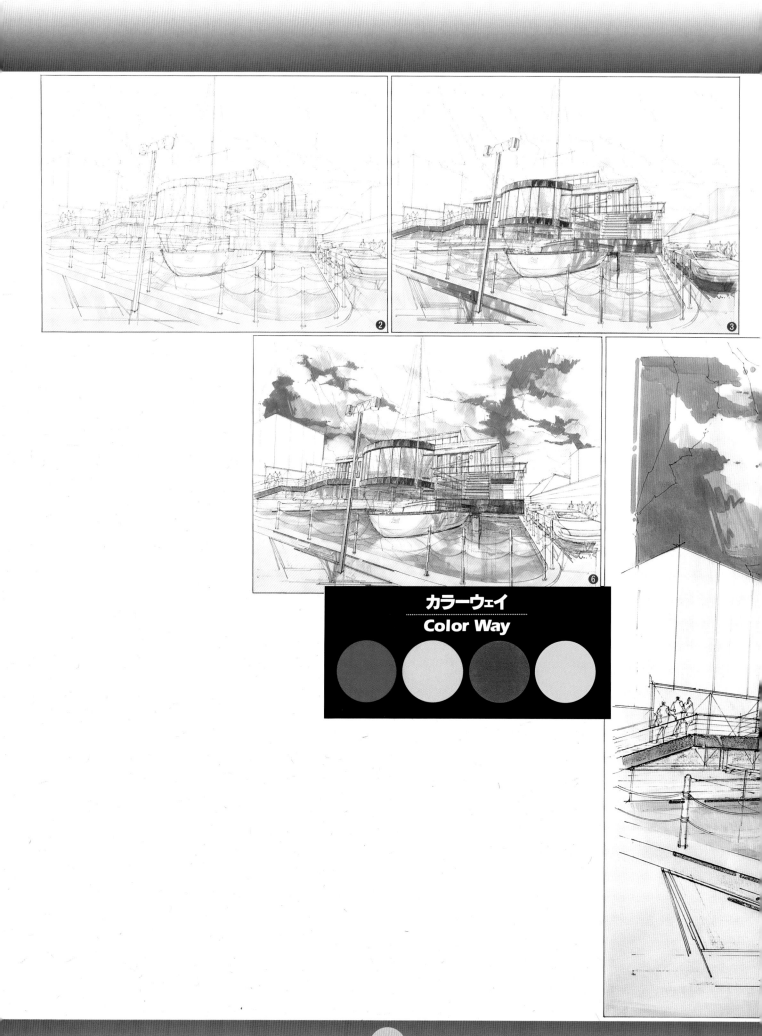

カラーウェイ
Color Way

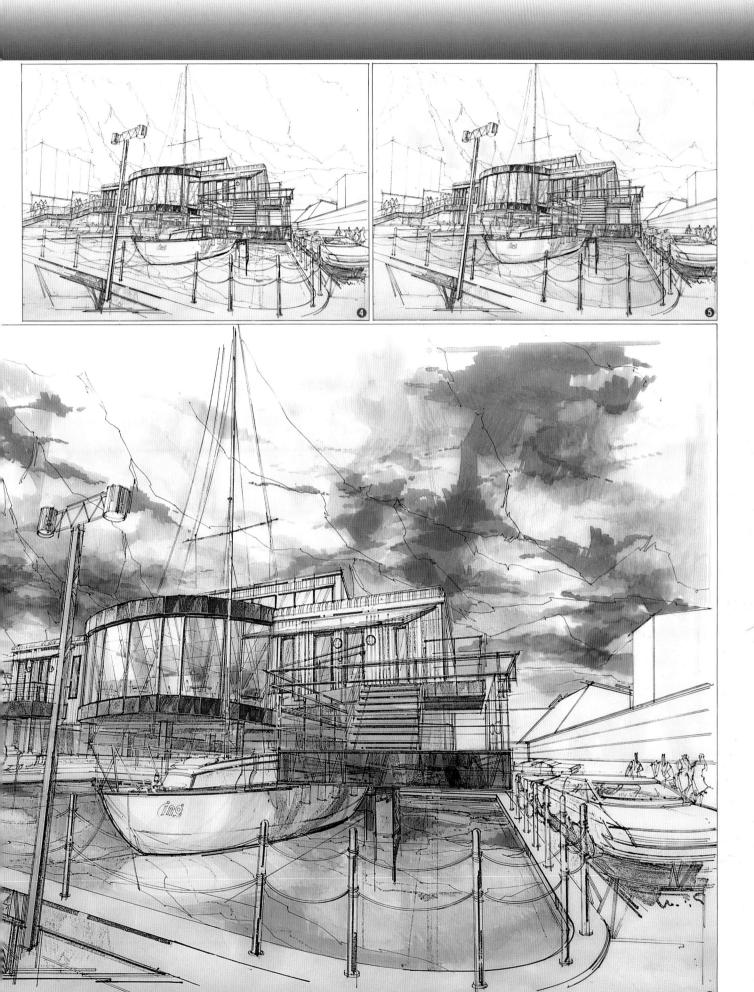

❶❷❸❹❺
墨入れ。
❻❼❽❾
下地の明暗を, グレーによるモノトーンで表現。
❿⓫
チントマーカーやカラーブレンドの使用により,
茶系どうしの質感の違いを描き込む。
⓬⓭
ガラスや金属, 人物などに色を入れる。
ポスターカラーのホワイトを点景やその他,
ハイライト部分のアクセントに使う。
いろいろなニュアンスで描き込むようにする。
⓮
完成である。

❶❷❸❹❺
Inking.
❻❼❽❾
Use monotones to express the grey shading
in the groundcoat.
❿⓫
Use tint markers and blended colors to draw
in the different qualities of the brown shaded
materials.
⓬⓭
Color in the glass, metal and people.

Use white poster color to draw in the various
nuances in the human and other high-life
accents.
⓮
The work is now complete.

使 用 マ ー カ ー
Markers used in the drawing.

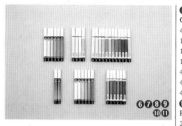

❻❼❽❾		319-M
Color blend		134-M
471 tint 10%-100%		475-M
132-M		250-M
140-M		243-M
162-M		251-M
471-M		176-M
484-M		170-M
497-M		Orange 021-M
❿⓫		265-M
Process cyan tint 10%-100%		Purple M
290-M		Rhodamine red M
304-M		Process yellow 2-M
317-M		

❻❼❽❾
❿⓫

このレストランの内, 外装の色は全体に茶系の濃淡で, わずかなガラス, 鉄の鋳物をのぞいては, だいたい茶系である。
その使用材料は石, 壁面の土壁, 床のタイル, そして木である。

Project 12 スペイン料理レストラン 内装
Spanish-style Restaurant Interior Decoration.

Shades of brown have been used on the entire interior color coordination of this restaurant. The materials used in the construction, such as stone, earthen walls, floor tiles and wood, are also more or less depicted in shades of brown with the exception of the small amount of glass and cast iron items used in some of the areas.

プロセス
Process

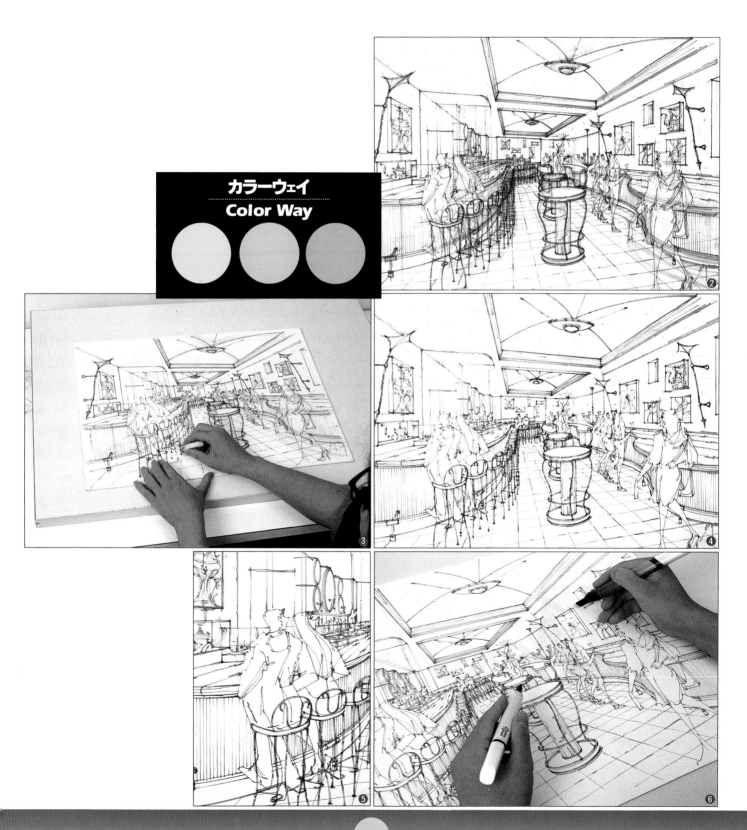

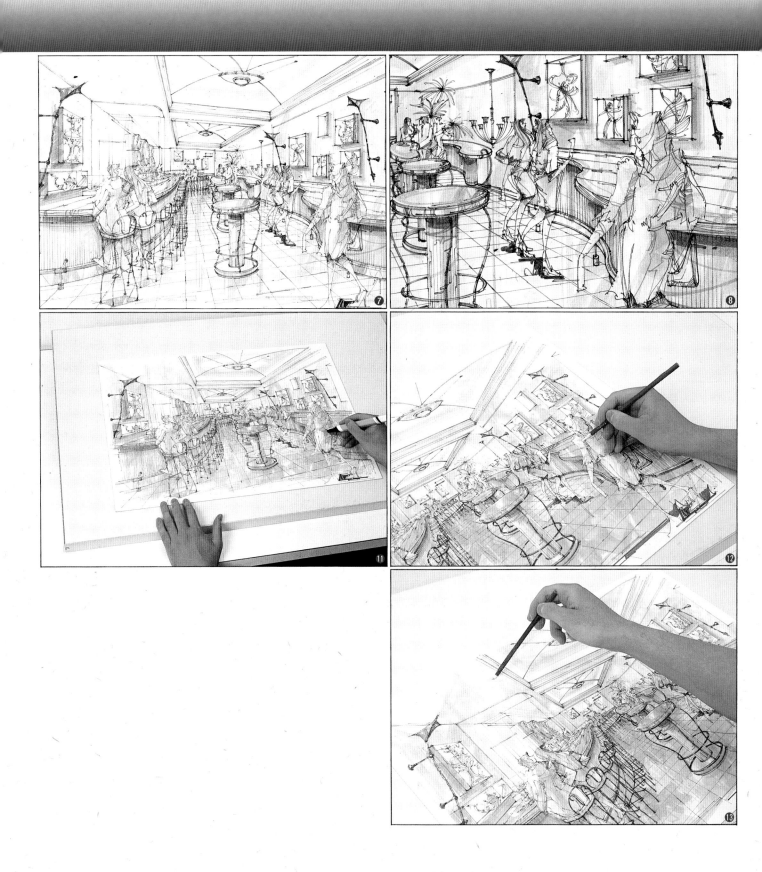

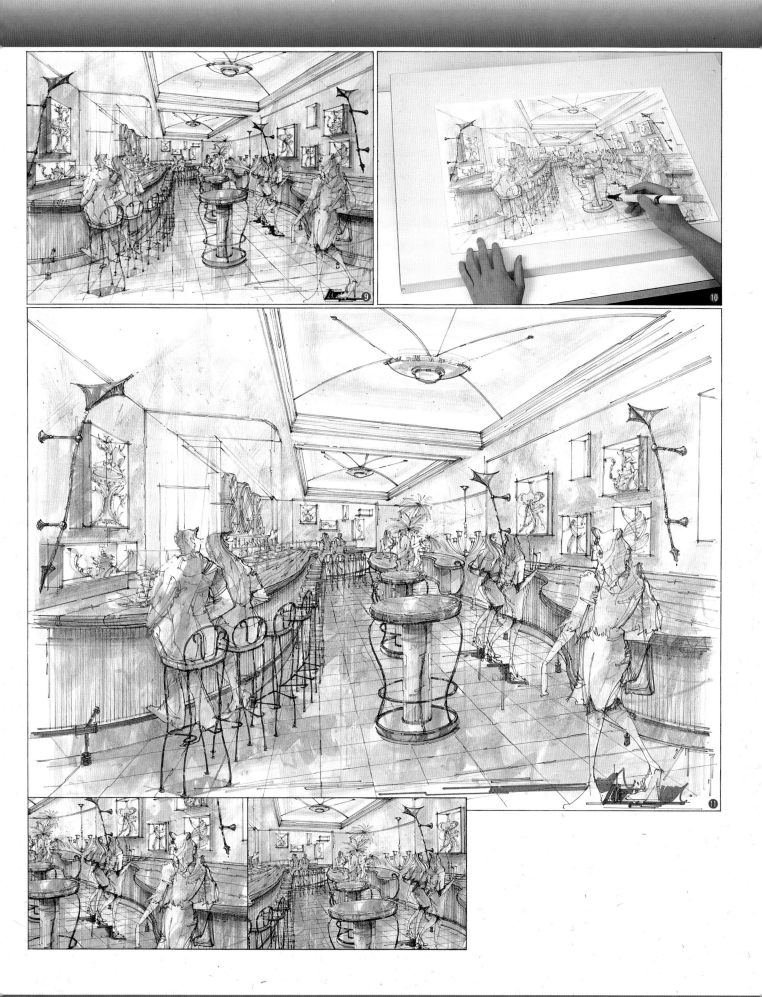

❶
墨入れ。
❷❸❹
明暗の濃淡をグレーでつける。
❺❻❼
茶系のバリエーションで, 質感を描き分ける。
木調のドア, 土壁, 石などである。
❽❾❿
ディスプレイ, 照明器具, 点景などに色を入れる。
⓫
完成である。

❶
Inking.
❷❸❹
Shades of grey.
❺❻❼
Draw in in the distinct quality of each
material by using variations of brown shades.
The wooden door, earthen wall and stone.
❽❾❿
Color in the display, lighting fixtures and
human items.
⓫
The work is now complete.

使 用 マ ー カ ー
Markers used in the drawing.

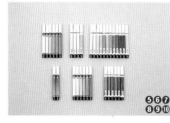

❺❻❼	319-M
Color blend	134-M
471 tint 10%-100%	475-M
132-M	250-M
140-M	243-M
162-M	251-M
471-M	176-M
484-M	170-M
497-M	Orange 021-M
❽❾❿	265-M
Process cyan tint 10%-100%	Purple M
290-M	Rhodamine red M
304-M	Process yellow 2-M
317-M	

❺❻❼
❽❾❿

外装のイメージは, スペイン料理レストラン 内装の延長である。

Project 13　スペイン料理レストラン 外装
Spanish-style Restaurant Exterior.

The exterior image in a continuation of the interior image.

プロセス
Process

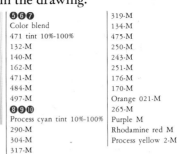

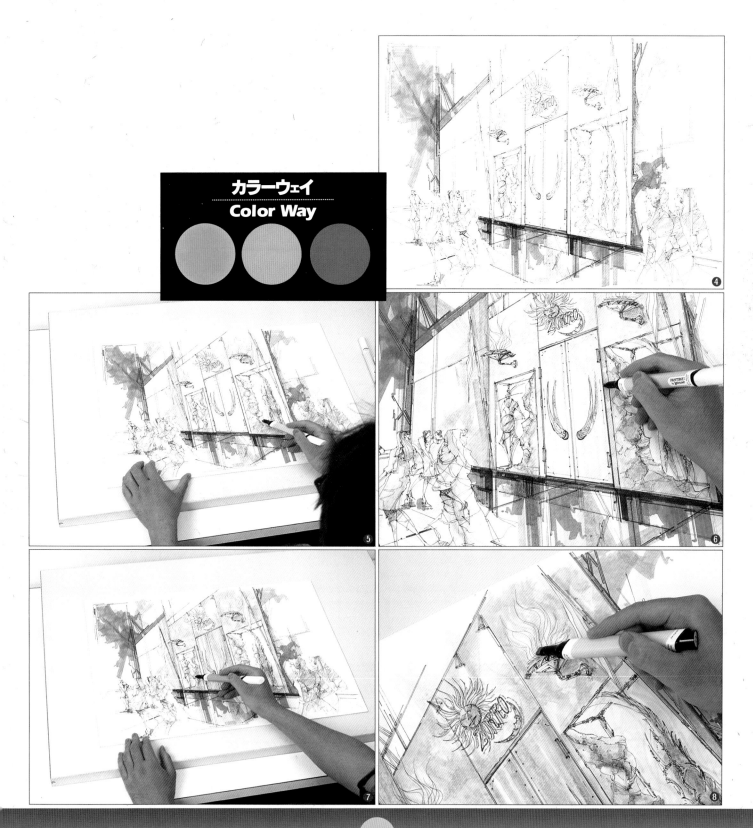

カラーウェイ
Color Way

モスク イメージ：a：MOSQUE IMAGE
アース・ファクトリー：b：Earth Factory
イスラムのモスクをイメージしたスケッチであるが，:d: This is an image sketch of an Islam-style mosque,
カスバのような路地，テントとそのすきまから見える　　but the point of the picture is the contrast of the mosque
モスクと空の抜けるような青さの対比。　　viewed through the opening between the alley and the tents,
着彩をあえてモスクとバックのブルーだけに絞り，　　so reminiscent of the Casbah, and the deep blue sky.
抜けるような空とブルーの色の画面上での構図との対比が　　The coloring has been restricted to the mosque
このスケッチのポイントである。　　and the blue sky of the background in order to create a contrast
空の回りのラインの流れと空の色面の対比により，　　between the blue and the composition of the sketch.
主と従のポイントを作る。　　The primary and secondary points are made by
giving contrast to the outline flows of the sky and the sky itself.

ディスコ ファサード・アーチ・イメージ：a：DISCOTHEQUE-FACADE ARCH IMAGE
アース・ファクトリー：b：Earth Factory
イスラムの廃虚風アーチ・イメージのディスコ。：d：An arch image of a ruined Islam-style discotheque.
バックの赤による彩色が，このスケッチのポイントのすべて。　The red background is the whole point of this sketch.
青や黄でなく赤にしたところにより，　Not blue on yellow, but red was chosen especially
このスケッチのドラマチック性を盛り上げている。　to increase the dramtic impression of the whole sketch.
また，赤のバックのタッチと画面のキワのタッチに　It is also important to add some nuance to the touches
ニュアンスをつけることがポイントである。　given to the background of red and the actual sketch.

レストラン&プール・イメージ：a：RESTAURANT & POOL IMAGE
アース・ファクトリー：b：Eerth Factory

スカンジナビア レストラン：a：SCANDINAVIA-RESTAURANT
アース・ファクトリー：b：Earth Factory

レストラン オーロラ：a：RESTAURANT-AURORA
アース・ファクトリー：b：Earth Factory

トロピカル・レストラン ボラ・ボラ : a : TROPICAL RESTAURANT-BORA BORA
アース・ファクトリー : b : Earth Factory
南海のトロピカル・レストランのポイントは、: d : The important point in drawing this southern sea
パステルトーンの色の流れを部分的ではなく tropical restaurant is to add strokes
画面全体に入れること。 of tropical-type pastel tone colors.
南海の色のかがやきを明るめの色彩により表現する。 Use bright colors to express the brightness of the south seas.

ディスコ 水上テラス・イメージ：a：DISCOTHEQUE-WATER TERRACE IMAGE
アース・ファクトリー：b：Earth Factory
ディスコを廃虚風に表現したファサードと：d：The ruined-style discotheque facade,
水上テラス・イメージ，そして空中階段，水面の広がり。　the water terrace image, the air stairs, and the extension of water.
黄色を中心とする色調の流れ，　The flow of the colors are based on yellow.
水の流れをおのおのの色の響きあいで表現。　The water flow is expressed by shades of each color.
水面，空間の中にただようように，　The colors should be painted on lightly
色彩もやわらかく表現したのがポイント。　as they are afloat in the water and air.

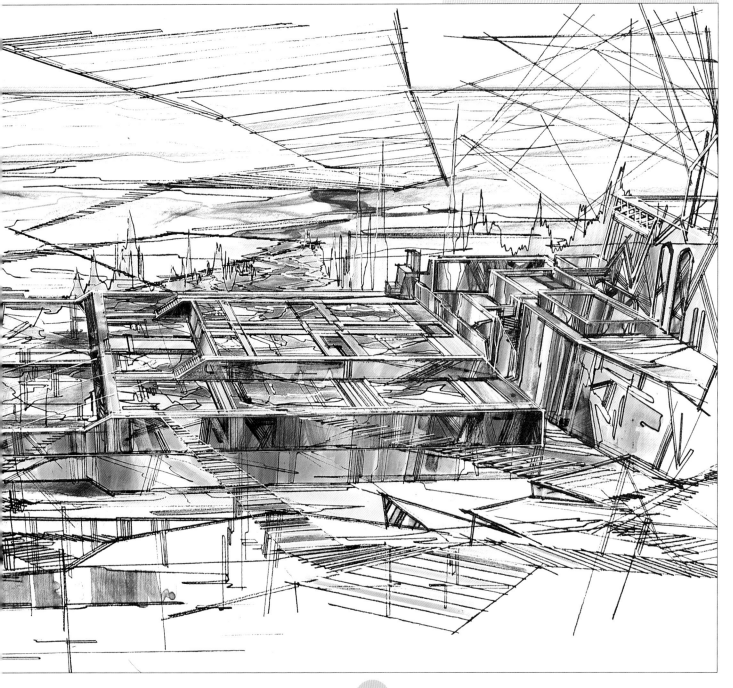

117

カフェ ジェニ・ジェニ：a：CAFE-JENNY JENNY
アース・ファクトリー：b：Earth Factory
レストランのファサードと：d：A flow of common color should be used
そのバックに共通の色の流れを作る。　in this restaurant facade and its background.
デザインが鋭角的なのでタッチもはぎれよく入れる。　Being designed with acute angles,
ガラスを基調として作られた店内も　the sketch should be painted with brisk strokes.
確実にしっかり描き込むのがポイント。　The details behind the glass should be drawn in rather precisely.
陰影の引き締め方により，画面にポイントとパンチを与える。　The addition of shadows will
give some punch to the sketch.

ライブ・ハウス ケントス：a：LIVE HOUSE-KENTOS
エム・ディー：b：M.D.Co.,Ltd.
エム・ディー：c：M.D.Co.,Ltd.

カフェ・ファサード：a：CAFE FACADE
アース・ファクトリー：b：Earth Factory

119

サンリオ ショップ・イメージ：a：SANRIO-SHOP IMAGE
サンリオ：c：Sanrio Co.,Ltd.

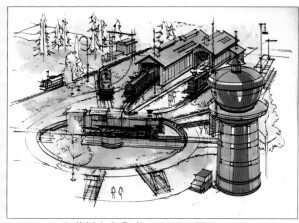

バンダイ トレインランド：**a**：BANDAI-TRAIN LAND
テツ・クリエイティブ：**b**：Tetsu Creative Co.,Ltd.
テツ・クリエイティブ：**c**：Tetsu Creative Co.,Ltd.

バンダイ トレインランド：**a**：BANDAI-TRAIN LAND
テツ・クリエイティブ：**b**：Tetsu Creative Co.,Ltd.
テツ・クリエイティブ：**c**：Tetsu Creative Co.,Ltd.

バンダイ トレインランド：**a**：BANDAI-TRAIN LAND
テツ・クリエイティブ：**b**：Tetsu Creative Co.,Ltd.
テツ・クリエイティブ：**c**：Tetsu Creative Co.,Ltd.

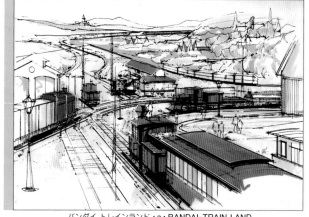

バンダイ トレインランド：**a**：BANDAI-TRAIN LAND
テツ・クリエイティブ：**b**：Tetsu Creative Co.,Ltd.
テツ・クリエイティブ：**c**：Tetsu Creative Co.,Ltd.

自然食レストラン：**a**：NATURAL FOOD RESTAURANT
アース・ファクトリー：**b**：Earth Factory

ディスコ アース・クエイク：**a**：DISCOTHEQUE-EARTH QUAKE
センチメンタル・シティ・スタジオ：**b**：Sentimental Sity Studio
センチメンタル・シティ・スタジオ：**c**：Sentimental Sity Studio

ジャカルタ ディスコ：a：DJAKARTA-DISCOTHEQUE
エアー・スタジオ：b：Air Studio

外装と違い内装はモノトーンの着彩で描く。：d：As opposed to the exterior color,
モノトーンにより質感のイメージをポイントに描く。　the color chosen for the interior is monotone.
このスケッチのもう一つのポイントは線である。　The main point should be placed
水性サインペンと面相筆による水墨画風な線のタッチ。　on the quality image of the monotone colors.
これは最上級のテクニックの一つでもある。　The other point in this sketch is the line.
それらのタッチをマーカーのタッチとからませて描く。　With the use of water color felt-tip pens and a fine brush,
　linesl touches should be added to produce an indian style of painting.
　This requires one of the highest techniques.
　These touches should be added with markers.

バンダイ ビル&レストラン : a : BANDAI-BUILDING & RESTAURANT
ポイントスタジオ : b : Point Studio
このスケッチのポイントは構図。: d : The important point of this sketch
手前はロボット・ジャズトリオ。can be summed up in a single word : composition.
右側にレストラン，中央にガラス製のカウンター・バー。It is a very exciting composition with a Robot jazz trio
天井には天の川の照明と，その天井の向う側に in the foreground, a restaurant on the right,
大天体望遠鏡の天文台というエキサイティングな空間構成である。a glass counter in the center, milky way style lighting
明暗のトーンの対比によりドラマチックな構図を演出する。on the ceiling and an astronomy observatory
with a telescope installed beyong the celing.
The contrasts of the tones have been
used to produce a very dramatic composition.

レストラン&カフェ フィニー：a：RESTAURANT & CAFE-FINY
コンセプト・キュー：b：Concept Q Co.,Ltd.
コンセプト・キュー：c：Concept Q Co.,Ltd.

バンダイ インフォメーション・コーナー：a：BANDAI-INFORMATION CORNER

バンダイ・ビル プール・イメージ：a：BANDAI BUILDING-POOL IMAGE

ファッション・ビル シーン：a：FASHION BUILDING-SEEN

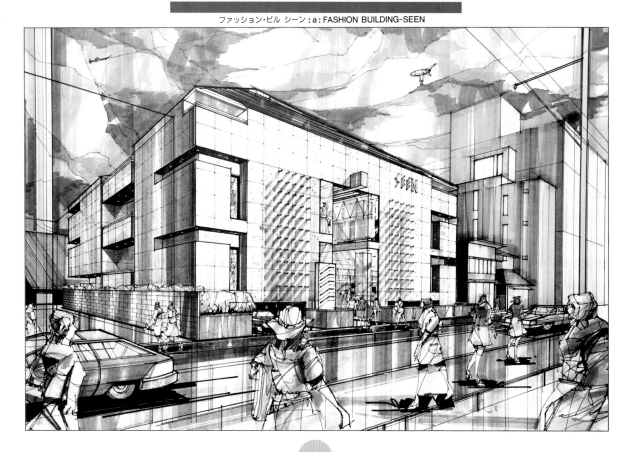

ファッション・ビル シーン：a：FASHION BUILDING-SEEN

リムジン・バー：**a**：LIMOUSINE BAR
松下電器産業，総合デザインセンター，エアー・スタジオ：**b**：Matsushita Electric Co.,Ltd., Sogo Design Center, Air Studio
松下電器産業，総合デザインセンター：**c**：Matsushita Electric Co.,Ltd., Sogo Design Center

リムジン・バー：**a**：LIMOUSINE BAR
松下電器産業，総合デザインセンター，エアー・スタジオ：**b**：Matsushita Electric Co.,Ltd., Sogo Design Center, Air Studio
松下電器産業，総合デザインセンター：**c**：Matsushita Electric Co.,Ltd., Sogo Design Center

ワールド・トラベル・フェアー :a: WORD TRAVEL FAIR
オムニバス，エアー・スタジオ :b: Omunibus, Air Studio
地球の白と回りのタッチの躍動感により， :d: The dramatic atmosphere of this space should be expressed
この空間のドラマチックさを演出する。 by the white earth and lively strokes around it.
地球の表面はレリーフのラインのみ。 Only relief lines have been drawn on the surface of the earth.
タッチはうすいグレーのみである。 Light grey alone should be used to
色をおさえ大きな画面全体のリズムを大切にする。 express the touches. The tone of the colors should be kept down,
and instead great care should be paid
to the rhythm of the entire sketch.

WORLD
TRAVEL
FAIR'84

ジャカルタ ディスコ：**a**：DJAKARTA-DISCOTHEQUE
エアー・スタジオ：**b**：Air Studio

ポストモダンとオリエンタルが：**d**：	This is an exterior design composed of
不思議なバランスで構成された外装デザイン。	an odd balance of postmodern and oriental designs.
表現のポイントは，明暗のトーンのダイナミズムである。	The expressional point is placed
空間の中に浮かび上がるファサードと	on the dynamic feeling of the light and dark tones.
バックの黒による画面の引き締め。	The facade should stand out in the space,
これにより空間のドラマチックなイメージを作り上げる。	and the use of black in the background should brace up the sketch.
	This will bring a dramatic image to the space.

カフェ：**a**：CAFE
株式会社リンク，三原実：**b**：Link Co.,Ltd., Minoru Mihara
株式会社リンク，三原実：**c**：Link Co.,Ltd., Minoru Mihara

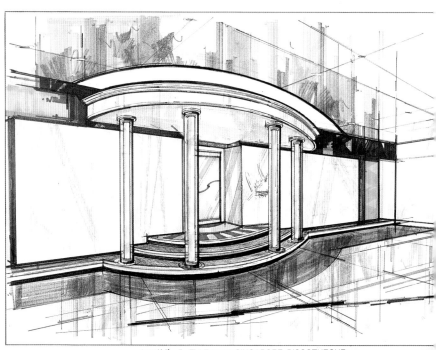

シンガポール ディスコ：**a**：SINGAPORE-DISCOTHEQUE
株式会社リンク，三原実：**b**：Link Co.,Ltd., Minoru Mihara

コンピュータ・ショップ 太郎・花子：**a**：COMPUTER SHOP-TARO & HANAKO
サン・アド：**b**：Sun AD Co.,Ltd.
キー・ステーション：**c**：Key Station Co.,Ltd.

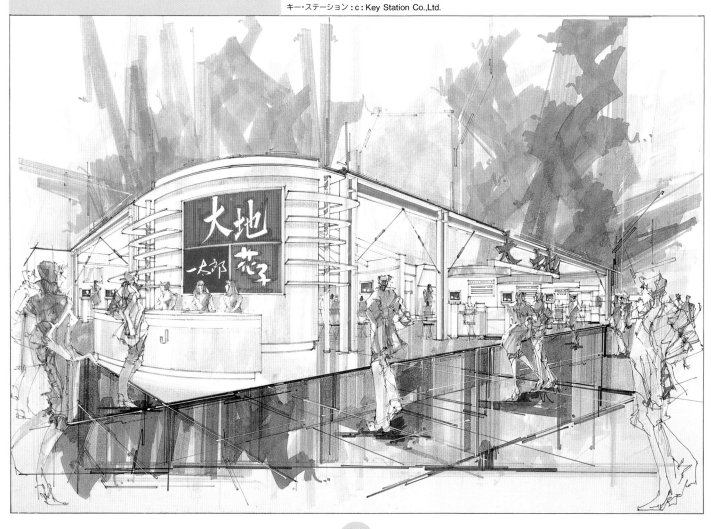

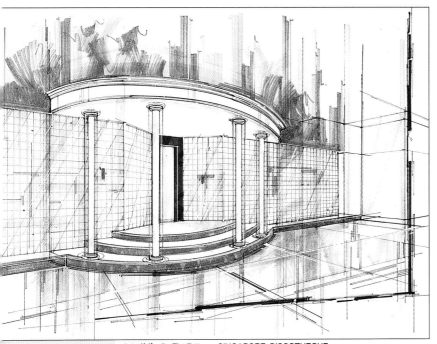

シンガポール ディスコ：**a**：SINGAPORE-DISCOTHEQUE
株式会社リンク，三原実：**b**：Link Co.,Ltd., Minoru Mihara

サントリー ワイン・ショップ：**a**：SUNTORY-WINE SHOP
サン・アド：**b**：Sun AD Co.,Ltd.
サントリー：**c**：Suntory Co.,Ltd.

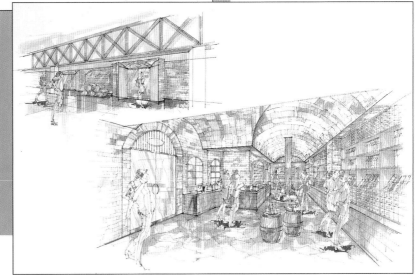

サントリー ワイン・ショップ：**a**：SUNTORY-WINE SHOP
サン・アド：**b**：Sun AD Co.,Ltd.
サントリー：**c**：Suntory Co.,Ltd.

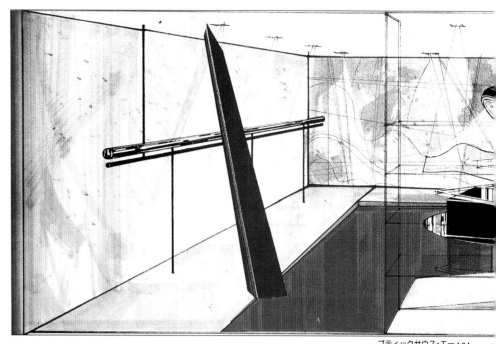

ブティックサウス・エー：a：
エアー・スタジオ，東京ソワール（岡奈保美）：b：
東京ソワール：c：
ロシア構成主義風の構成と色彩によるブティック。：d：
色彩はロシア構成主義風の渋い赤，渋い紺がポイント。
中央のステージ上部の照明は，病院の手術用照明器具。
左側の渋い紺のイメージのオブジェが
空間の赤に対するポイントである。
導線は回廊風なデザイン。
キャンソンボードにマーカーの色を塗り込むように彩色していく。

シンガポール ディスコ：a：SINGAPORE-DISCOTHEQUE
株式会社リンク，三原実：b：Link Co.,Ltd., Minoru Mihara

シンガポール ディスコ：a：SINGAPORE-DISCOTHEQUE
株式会社リンク，三原実：b：Link Co.,Ltd., Minoru Mihara

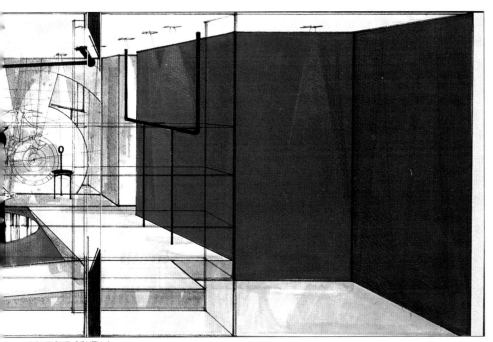

BOUTIQUE-SOUTH A
Air Studio, Tokyo Sowar Co.,Ltd.(Naomi Oka)
Tokyo Sowar Co.,Ltd.
A boutique with a strictly Russian style of composition.
The emphasis on the colors goes to
somber Russian red and navy blue.
The lighting fixture over the stage is the same
as that used in hospital operating theaters.
The navy blue object makes a point against the red in the space.
The marker colors of the boards seem as if have been popped in.

シンガポール ディスコ：a：SINGAPORE-DISCOTHEQUE
株式会社リンク，三原実：b：Link Co.,Ltd., Minoru Mihara

シンガポール ディスコ：a：SINGAPORE-DISCOTHEQUE
株式会社リンク，三原実：b：Link Co.,Ltd., Minoru Mihara

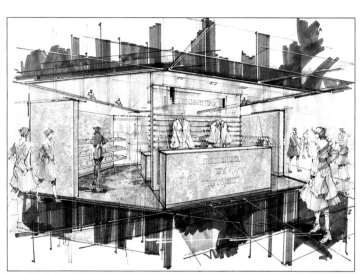

ブティック シンセンドー : a : BOUTIQUE-SINSENDO

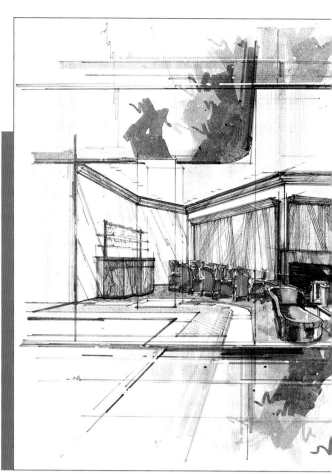

シンガポール ディスコ : a : SINGAPORE-DISCOTHEQUE
株式会社リンク，三原実 : b : Link Co.,Ltd., Minoru Mihara

レストラン 鬼の隠れ場：a：RESTAURANT ONI-NO-KAKUREBA
エアー・スタジオ：b：Air Studio

スペイン レストラン：a：SPAIN-RESTAURANT

レストラン 鬼の隠れ場：a：RESTAURANT ONI-NO-KAKUREBA
エアー・スタジオ：b：Air Studio

北の家族：a：KITA-NO-KAZOKU
和田裕設計室：b：Yutaka Wada Space Planning Office
北の家族：c：Kita-no-kazoku Co.,Ltd.

レストラン 彩(さい)：a：RESTAURANT SAI
エアー・スタジオ：b：Air Studio

第四章
コピーフリーの
点景ファイル集
Copyright-free Spot Images.
Chapter 4

138

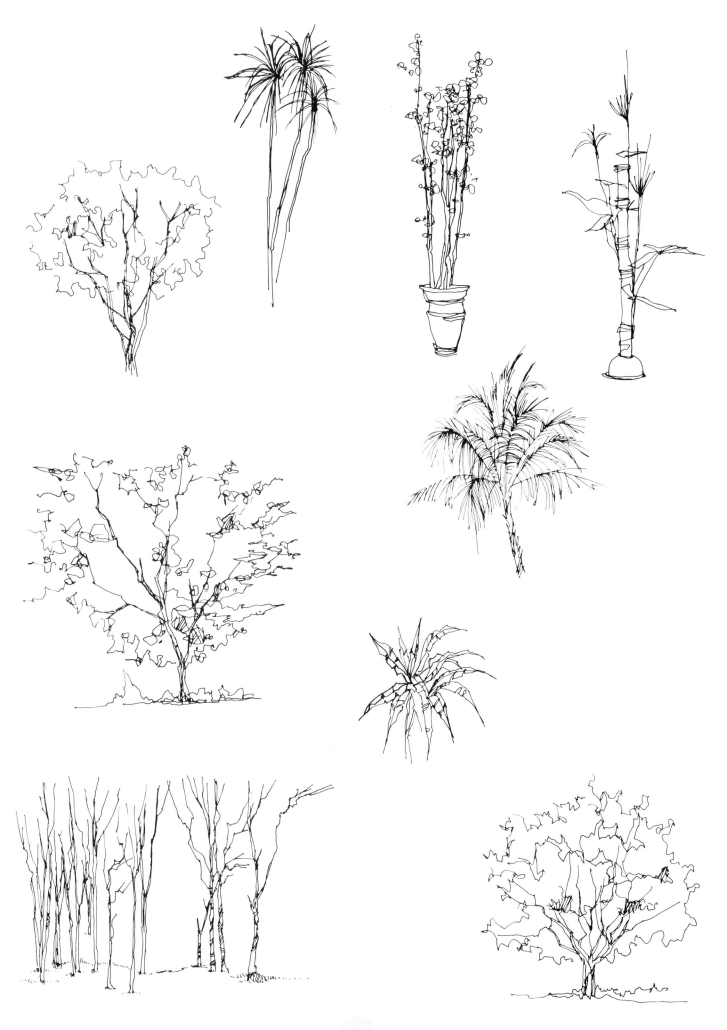

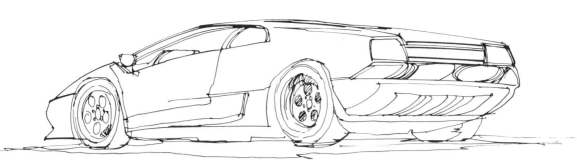

あ
と
が
き

マーカーを中心としたスペースレンダリングのテクニック書を作りたいと，グラフィック社編集部の大田氏より話があったとき，軽く返事をしてしまったのはいいが，このときが後悔の始りでもあった。実は私のテクニックは，マーカーや筆，その他の画材を単純に動作させる連続作業で，その単純な作業のバックボーンである画面構成が私のテクニックの全てである事に気が付いたのである。この事はマーカーの持つ画材としての使いやすさから来るもので，個々のテクニックをこと細かに解説しなくても誰でも描ける画材であったということの証明である。さらに，印刷された自分の作品を見て，画面構成の重要さに改めて気が付いたりもした。四苦八苦の作業だったが，結果として私自身が一番楽しんだのかもしれない。
本書を作成するにあたり，巻頭企画『感性のダイレクト表現』をご寄稿頂いたミサワホーム株式会社の三澤千代治社長，何千枚という写真を撮影してくれたカメラマンの小堀晃通氏(スタジオ・クアルト)，そして私のわがままを聞き入れながら美しいデザインをしてくれたブックデザイナーの箕浦卓氏，グラフィック社編集部の大田悟氏，そしてこの本のために協力してくれたスタッフやブレーンの皆さんに感謝するしだいです。本当にありがとうございました。

安土実(………あづちみのる)
エアー・スタジオ代表：
東京都渋谷区本町6-2-21
メゾンヒロ201 〒151
電話：03〈3378〉6126

When Mr.Ota from the editorial department of Graphic-sha, approached me to ask if I could compile a technical book on space rendering using markers, I simply accepted without considering it too deeply. This was, I learned later, a big mistake. To tell the truth, I do not consider myself in posession of any special techniques when it comes to markers, brushes or any other tools. To me it is simply a series of work. I discovered that my technique lies in the composition of a picture which is the backbone of all simple work. This proves that markers can be handled by anybody without having previously been supplied with any specific details as to technique. Looking at my finished work in print, I reconfirmed that the most important part of a picture is the composition. It was a bit of struggle, but as a result, I believe it was me who enjoyed it most.

I would like to offer my deepest thanks to Mr.Chiyoji Misawa, a president of Misawa Homes Co., Ltd. who contributed an essay with the title of "Direct Impression of One's Sense", as well as Mr.Kobori **(STUDIO QUARTO)**, the cameraman who spent so much time taking over 1000 photographs, Mr.Minoura, the designer who was patient enough to listen to my demands and come up with such beautiful designs, Mr.Ota from the editorial department of Graphic-sha Publishing Co.,Ltd., and all the staff who gave the benefit of their aid in order to publish this book. Thank you all.

Minoru Azuchi
AIR STUDIO:
Maison Hiro #201, 6-2-21
Honchyo, Shibuya-ku, Tokyo, 151
Tel.: 03〈3378〉6126

Afterword

スペース・レンダリング

建築マーカー・テクニック

Step-by-Step
Architectural Marker Techniques

初版第1刷発行
1991年5月25日

著　者
安土実

撮　影
小堀晃通

装　丁
箕浦卓

レイアウト
箕浦卓

翻　訳
株式会社新世社

画材協力
レトラセットジャパン株式会社

発行者
久世利郎

印　刷
錦明印刷株式会社

製　本
錦明印刷株式会社

写　植
三和写真工芸株式会社

デザイン印字
井上聖昭

発　行
株式会社グラフィック社
〒102 東京都千代田区九段北1-9-12
Tel.03-3263-4318

乱丁・落丁はお取り替え致します。

ISBN4-7661-0638-5 C3052